Bulgarian Cuisine

Sofia, Bulgaria
May 6, 2002
St. George's Day

May Publishing House
Sofia

Dimitar Mantov

Bulgarian Cuisine

The best traditional recipes

May Publishing House
Sofia

Measures

It is easier to measure the ingredients with spoons and cups. Here is the approximate capacity of some of them:

1 level tablespoon = 15 ml milk or water, 10 g flour, 15 g sugar, 12 ml oil, 18 g rice, 20 g salt

1 level teaspoon = 5 ml milk or water, 3 g flour, 4 g sugar, 5 ml oil, 5 g rice, 5 g salt

1 (tea) cup = 200 ml milk or water, 120 g flour, 150 g sugar, 180 ml oil, 180 g rice, 180 g salt.

1 coffee cup = 80 ml water or milk, 50 g flour, 60 g sugar, 60 ml oil, 70 g rice, 70 g salt

1 pinch = the quantity you get with thumb and first two fingers

1 medium potato = 130 g

1 medium tomato = 100 g

1 medium onion = 50 g

1 egg = 50 g

1 coffee cup = 1/2 (tea) cup

1 glass = 200 ml

Contents

Introduction

Nearly five thousand recipes which have survived for five thousand years until the present: that is traditional Bulgarian cuisine. I have been collecting Bulgaria's culinary treasures for thirty five years, and thanks to my good cooperation with *May* Publishing House, Sofia, most of them, 4,500, have been published. Those offered in the present book are specially selected and tested: they are the most typical ones and easy to prepare.

Some of the oldest recipes are inherited from the Thracians who, together with the proto-Bulgarians and Slavs, formed the Bulgarian nation. The main holidays during the year are Thracian with the exception of a proto-Bulgarian one and a Slavic one.

The Christian religion adopted the pagan holidays: for instance, the holiday of the cheerful Thracian God Dionysos (which the ancient Greeks borrowed and declared their god) is called Trifon Zarezan and is celebrated on February 1; the big spring holiday dedicated to the Thracian Hero-rider is called Gergyovden (celebrated on May 6). It is the first day of each year when people eat lamb. There is special ritual food for each holiday: meat from an animal offered as a sacrifice in the past, and ritual bread called *pogacha*. The first chickens raised during the year are cooked on St. Peter's Day (June 29). In many towns and villages there are fairs on that day. On St. Nicolas' Day (December 6) people cook fish, on Christmas – pork from a pig, specially raised for that holiday.

The **first** peculiarity of the Bulgarian traditional cuisine is its seasonal character. This is due to the local climatic conditions, the work and everyday life of the Bulgarians.

The seasonal character of Bulgarian cooking leads to its **second** peculiarity, namely the use of fresh products and the combination of various kinds of meat with vegetables, typical for each individual season.

For instance, lamb is mainly cooked with parsley, green onions or spinach. Pork is cooked with beans or sour cabbage, mutton – with tomatoes or potatoes, veal – with plums, chicken – with green onions.

The **third** peculiarity is the wide variety of products: lots of vegetables, mushrooms, beans, peas, lentils, different kinds of fruit and meat, snails, fish, rabbits and hares. Game is cooked according to ancient, tested recipes and marinated beforehand with typical local products.

The **fourth** peculiarity is that each product is cooked with a specific kind of fat: vegetable oil or olive oil is used for vegetable dishes, and animal fat, butter or lard is used when cooking meat.

When cooking poultry (turkeys, hens, geese) it is recommended that only their own fat be used for better taste.

Lard is purified by boiling it with milk and various fruits until it becomes snow-white and fragrant. It is used for cooking various kinds of meat, poultry, game, and typical pastry products, like cheese pie (*banitsa*). Potatoes fried in purified lard are very tasty.

The **fifth** peculiarity is the great variety of spices used in cooking. In every Bulgarian region there are typical herbs and spices, not known in others. For instance, the plant called *smardala* (Thracian word) grows only in the vicinity of the city of Sliven, the region of the Strandzha mountains and the city of Stara Zagora. It is used (together with other spices) to make *spicy salt (sharena sol)*. In the regions of the cities Tryavna and Veliko Turnovo they use *taros* (tarragon) when cooking bean, chicken or fish soup, while in Shumen they often use the *levurda* (wild garlic) which grows there.

The **sixth** characteristic feature is the cooking technique:

Stewed dishes are cooked with a very small quantity of liquid. Thus the products preserve their juices and specific fragrance.

When cooking *kebap* you half-boil, half-stew meat and it remains more juicy than in stews (whose usual ingredients are onions and red pepper), although there is less sauce. Meat in this dish is more tasty and fragrant if you cut it in 2 cm cubes, place it in a marinade prepared from finely chopped onion, ground black pepper, savoury and a very small quantity of white wine or vinegar, and leave it for five-six hours in a cool place or in a covered pan in the refrigerator. For this dish one should choose meat from the leg and shoulder.

Gyuvech is a dish named after the big shallow ceramic casserole in which it is baked in the oven. It can be substituted by a baking pan or a fireproof glass pan. Typical for the this dish is that the ingredients are baked together but before that are lightly browned or boiled. Meat mainly from the front part of the animal: neck, breast and shoulder, is best for *gyuvech*. It is more suitable because it is streaked with fat and is also good for stews. Flour is not used when lightly browning the products, there is less sauce and at the end of baking the liquid is fully absorbed. *Gyuvech* is baked in a slow oven.

Kapama is a dish cooked with or without meat, with the addition of green onions. It simmers in a covered saucepan (*kapama* comes from *kapak*, which is Bulgarian for lid). It is made of different kinds of meat or of a combination of meats. You can prepare it from various vegetables, too.

A Christian fast (or lent) is observed several times throughout the year for religious, moral and health reasons. It has had an impact on the Bulgarian cuisine and has resulted in a wide variety of vegetable soups and dishes cooked without oil or animal proteins. During the fast they prepare snails, crabs, mussels and other mollusks, caviar etc. In the monasteries they also cook a lot of dishes with mushrooms and fresh vegetables.

Very often Bulgarians serve *banitsa* for breakfast, hot from the oven. It is made of phyllo dough with different stuffing. Traditionally, Bulgarians serve *boza* (millet-ale) with it.

Usually, Bulgarians serve meat dishes for lunch, while for dinner they eat milk and dairy products. Bulgarian yogurt is famous all over the world. It is said that it is the reason for Bulgarians' longevity. The Bulgarian white cheese, *sirene*, is very similar to Greek *feta* cheese and is made of sheep's, cow's or goat's milk. It is also gaining popularity among the numerous kinds of cheese in other European countries. The same is also true for *kashkaval*, typical Bulgarian hard yellow cheese. In Bulgarian cooking it can be substituted with any hard yellow cheese.

Bulgarians have preferences for certain kinds of meat during the different seasons: in spring they eat lamb, in summer – chicken and weaned lamb, in the fall – veal and mutton , and in winter – pork, wild boar, ducks and geese.

It is believed that river fish is the most delicious kind. Ranking first is the trout, especially when it is caught in fast-running mountain rivers. Mountain barbel is also a delicious river mountain fish. A lot of specialties can be cooked from Danube fish. The quality of Black Sea fish is close to that of freshwater fish because the Black Sea is closed.

In Bulgarian cuisine ground meat is made of 2/3 veal and 1/3 pork. One rarely uses just ground lamb or ground pork.

The internal parts, head and limbs of the animals are also part of the typical Bulgarian cooking.

One peculiarity of Bulgarian cuisine is the use of ceramic casseroles for cooking and baking. The food cooked in such a casserole or a pot tastes much better, because these casseroles are heated up more slowly and cooking takes place over moderate heat. The big ceramic casserole is called *gyuvech*, and the small one for individual serving – *gyuveche*. They can be with or without lids. Ceramic dishes can be substituted by fireproof glass ones.

Well-prepared Bulgarian food looks very appetizing – the meat is baked in the oven until covered with golden-brown crust. The *gyuvech* is topped with sliced tomatoes and looks very attractive. You can also pour a mixture made of beaten eggs with chopped parsley over it, which is baked for several more minutes and makes a delicious golden crust. A similar mixture can also be poured over other dishes: both vegetable ones and those with meat. For soups Bulgarians use milk or yogurt thickeners with or without beaten eggs.

Typical Bulgarian specialties are offered at many restaurants, especially at the folk taverns, called *mehana*. Very often the restaurants serve typical local dishes, for instance that of the Rhodope mountains, Pirin, Strandzha mountains, the Balkan Range, etc. The wine served with the food can be white or red, dry or semi-dry, sweet, ordinary or sparkling. According to the tradition, white wine should be fragrant, and red should be thick and bright. The flavor of the wine depends on the climate and soil in the region where it was made, on the variety of grapes, the way they were gathered, the fermentation technology, the wood of the casks in which the wine was aged. Many of the grape varieties in Bulgaria were originally imported and later adapted to the local conditions. Red wine is very popular in this country. It is praised in the folk songs. The legend says that some of the best varieties such as: Mavrud, Melnik, Gamza, were preferred even by Krali Marko, a beloved hero in the Bulgarian folk tales.

One should also give due consideration to the Bulgarian brandy, *rakiya*, which is a product of distillation of grapes or other fruits, plums being among the preferred ones. Plum brandy is called *slivovitsa*.

One should be careful about *mastika*, a specific aniseed alcoholic drink which is very strong and should be diluted with a fair amount of water.

In cold weather Bulgarians prefer to have *rakiya*, warmed up with some honey or caramelized sugar, or wine, sweetened and warmed up with various spices, most often cloves.

Another typical Bulgarian refreshment is yogurt diluted with mineral water and seasoned with salt. It is called *airan* or *mutenitsa*, and is served cold. The millet-ale (*boza*) is typical for the whole Balkan region.

The recipes in this book are true to the Bulgarian culinary tradition. Many of them come from the remote past, but even today they are alive and cooked in different guises in Bulgarian homes, restaurants and taverns.

Of course, Bulgarian cuisine has been influenced by the cuisine of many neighbouring and other nations, and is not what it used to be in the past. The most popular tripe soup shares a peaceful coexistence with the exotic Chinese, Mexican, Arab and other foods, not to mention the inevitable hamburgers, cheeseburgers, pizza, hot-dogs, etc.

However, being acquainted in detail with the Bulgarian dishes and drinks, one will have an additional choice in the future.

For us, making this decision will be easy, because we know from experience that healthy Bulgarian food (guarantee for long life) is the reason for the large number of centenarians in this country. And a glass of high-quality wine is always good for the health.

Salads and Appetizers

SHARENA SOL
(SPICY SALT)

It is available in every Bulgarian home. Sometimes, warm round bread (*pitka*) is served with spicy salt as an appetizer. In some regions *sharena sol* is called *pepper salt*, because red pepper is one of its main ingredients. Red pepper can be prepared at home.

To make red pepper: Slightly roast 15–20 dry red peppers in a moderate oven. Crush them in a wooden mortar, 4–5 at a time. Sprinkle pepper with oil and let dry in the sun or in a slow oven until bright red.

The following INGREDIENTS are needed to make *sharena sol*:

1 cup baked unpopped popcorn, 1 coffee cup walnuts,
3/4 cup crushed dried savoury,
1/2 teaspoon ground black pepper,
2 tablespoons mild red pepper, 1 tablespoon salt

PREPARATION:
1. Crush baked unpopped popcorn in a wooden mortar.
2. Place walnuts in a dry baking pan. Lightly bake them in a moderate oven (15 minutes or less). Crush in a mortar and combine with crushed popcorn and rubbed dried savoury.
3. Sift mixture through a coarse sieve or rub with hands. Discard bigger pieces and crush again. Coffee grinder can also be used for this purpose.
4. Combine these three ingredients with ground black pepper and mild red pepper. Add salt just before serving, because it is highly hygroscopic and easily becomes moist.
5. *Sharena sol* should be stored in a dry place in a glass jar with a tight lid. Use it when preparing sandwiches, meat balls or home-made sausage, or when cooking stews.

SHOPSKA SALAD

INGREDIENTS:
4 big (or 6 medium) tomatoes, 1 small (or 1/2 big) chopped onion,
1 medium cucumber, 4–5 peppers,
4 tablespoons oil, 1 tablespoon vinegar,
4 coffee cups grated sirene (white cheese),
4 chili peppers, 1 tablespoon parsley leaves, salt

1. Cut in small cubes tomatoes and peeled cucumber.
2. Stem and seed peppers, cut in thin long strips, add to chopped onion. Combine and sprinkle with salt, oil and vinegar.
3. Divide the salad in 4 small plates. Toss with grated cheese to form a pyramid. Stick one chili pepper in each one and garnish with parsley leaves.

KYUOPOOLU
(AUBERGINE CAVIARE)

INGREDIENTS:
1 medium bulb garlic, 3 tablespoons oil, 5–6 peppers,
4 medium aubergines, 2 tomatoes,
1/2 teaspoon salt of lemon, 2 tablespoons chopped parsley,
4–5 walnut kernels, 1 coffee cup crumbled sirene (white cheese), salt

1. Peel garlic and crush cloves to a pulp with a little salt in a wooden mortar. Pour in oil drop by drop, stirring with the pestle.
2. Roast and peel peppers (See Roast peppers salad). Stem and seed them, then chop and place in mortar. Beat mixture well with the pestle in one direction only, the way one beats caviar.
3. Bake aubergines in a hot oven or on a hot plate, turning them when the skin is well roasted on one side. (Sometimes they burst, so do not get alarmed.) You will know when they are done by finding them soft to touch. Let them cool. Skin by dipping the fingers in water as to be able to take away every bit of black skin (which sometimes gets burnt). Put pulp on a plate and tilt it slightly to let all the juice run off. Then place on a wooden board and chop with a knife. Put in mortar and beat well with pestle.

4. At the end add the blanched, peeled and chopped tomatoes. Beat mixture with the pestle until well blended and smooth.

5. Season with salt and salt of lemon diluted with some water. At the end add chopped parsley and crushed walnut kernels. Add some crumbled sirene (optional) and mix well with aubergine puree.

GREEN SALAD WITH EGGS

INGREDIENTS:
2–3 lettuces, 2 tablespoons chopped parsley,
2 tablespoons oil, 1 tablespoon vinegar, 1 tablespoon water,
1 teaspoon mustard, 1/4 kg drained yogurt,
2 hard-boiled eggs, salt

1. Tear lettuce in big pieces, add finely chopped parsley. Blend salt, oil, vinegar, water and mustard. Pour over lettuce.

2. Put 400 g yogurt in a cheesecloth pouch. Hang it in a convenient place and let the yogurt drain for 6 hours. (A big strainer, covered with filter paper or cheesecloth, can be used instead).

3. Divide the salad in 4 plates, top with drained yogurt, garnish with egg wedges.

TOMATO AND CUCUMBER SALAD

INGREDIENTS:
1 cucumber, 3 tomatoes, 1 onion,
2 peppers, 1/2 teaspoon ground black pepper,
2 teaspoons oil, 2 teaspoons vinegar,
2–3 leaves fresh basil, salt

1. Cut in cubes tomatoes and cucumbers.

2. Add onion, thinly sliced, and pepper, cut in thin rings.

3. Sprinkle with salt and ground black pepper. Toss with oil and vinegar, garnish with chopped basil leaves.

ROAST PEPPERS SALAD

INGREDIENTS:

10–12 peppers, parsley sprigs,
fresh savoury leaves, 2 tablespoons vinegar,
1 tablespoon chopped parsley, salt

For better taste use green instead of red peppers.

1. Roast peppers on strongly heated hot plate turning them round until they are completely covered with brown blisters. As soon as one is ready, take it off, put it in a basin and leave it to cool with a cover on. While peppers are still warm, dip fingers in cold water and peel off the blistered skin.

2. Split tips of peppers, put 2 sprigs of parsley in each, several savoury leaves and a pinch of salt.

3. Arrange peppers in a big plate. Cover with vinegar, thinned with some water. Let stay for 3–4 hours.

4. Before serving toss with oil and finely chopped parsley.

TOMATO SALAD

INGREDIENTS:

1/2 kg firm ripe tomatoes, 5–6 cloves garlic,
1 tablespoon oil,
1 tablespoon finely chopped parsley,
100 g grated sirene (white cheese)

1. Slice tomatoes and arrange in 4 small plates.

2. Crush garlic with a pinch of salt. Combine with parsley and oil and cover tomatoes. Top with grated cheese.

LYUTENITSA
(PEPPER-TOMATO PUREE)

INGREDIENTS:
750 g red peppers, 3 tomatoes,
3 tablespoons chopped parsley, 1 chili pepper,
1 coffee cup oil, vinegar, salt

1. Roast peppers and peel them (See Roast peppers salad). Remove seeds. Cut in small pieces.
2. Skin and grate tomatoes (to puree, use meat grinder or blender). Combine with peppers.
3. Mix with salt and vinegar to taste, chopped parsley and oil. Add one chili pepper, finely chopped (optional).
4. Serve the puree immediately or pour it into jars and sterilize for 10 minutes to use when required.
Served garnished with chopped onions.

GARLIC PUREE (CAVIAR)

INGREDIENTS:
2 bulbs garlic, 1 1/2 coffee cups oil, 1/3 teaspoon salt of lemon,
1 slice stale white bread, 5–6 walnut kernels,
1/2 tablespoon chopped parsley, salt

1. Peel garlic cloves, mince and puree in a wooden mortar with a little salt. Beat garlic puree with a wooden spoon.
2. In about 10 minutes start adding oil very gradually, continuing to beat mixture well.
3. When the puree becomes smooth and creamy, add salt of lemon diluted with some water.
4. Soak bread in water for some time, squeeze dry. Crush walnut kernels. Combine puree with bread, kernels and chopped parsley.

OLIVE PASTE

INGREDIENTS:
30–40 olives, 3 hard-boiled eggs, 1 onion,
2 teaspoons lemon juice

1. Pit olives. Pound in a wooden mortar, then transfer to a bowl.
2. In the same mortar pound the diced eggs. Add to olives.
3. Add grated onions.
4. Combine with lemon juice (or salt of lemon diluted with some water).

SNEZHANKA SALAD
(CUCUMBER-YOGURT SALAD)

INGREDIENTS:
1/2 kg cucumbers, 1 kg drained yogurt,
4–5 cloves garlic, 1/2 cup finely chopped parsley (or dill),
salt, 3 tablespoons oil

1. Pour 1 1/2 kg of yogurt into a cheesecloth pouch. Hang in a convenient place and let drain for 6 hours. (A big strainer covered with filter paper or cheesecloth can be used instead).
2. Peel cucumbers, dice, sprinkle with salt and lay aside so that the juice can run off.
3. Drain cucumbers in a strainer and combine with drained yogurt.
4. Crush garlic with a pinch of salt. Add oil and garlic to yogurt-cucumber mixture, stir well.

BAKED ONIONS SALAD

INGREDIENTS:
4 medium onions, 1 tablespoon vinegar, 1 tablespoon oil,
1/2 teaspoon ground black pepper, salt,
1 tablespoon chopped parsley

1. Choose firm medium onions. Place in a pan and bake in a moderate oven until tender. Peel.

2. The salad can be prepared also in another way: peel and cook the whole onions in a small quantity of water.

3. Place in a deep dish. Blend vinegar and oil. Pour over onions. Sprinkle with salt to taste, black pepper and chopped parsley.

LETTUCE SALAD

INGREDIENTS:

2 lettuces, 10 olives, 1 hard-boiled egg,

1/4 kg drained yogurt,

1 tablespoon chopped parsley, 1 tablespoon oil, salt

1. Set aside the small inside white lettuce leaves. Cut rest of leaves into thin strips. Place in the center of a big serving plate.

2. Arrange the small leaves around them. Put an olive or an egg edge in each.

3. Combine lettuce strips in the center of plate with chopped green onions (optional).

4. The salad can also be garnished with sliced radishes or with several spinach leaves.

5. Sprinkle lettuce with salt. Combine drained yogurt (See Green salad with eggs) with oil and chopped parsley. Pour over salad.

WHITE BEANS SALAD

INGREDIENTS:

1 cup beans, 2 onions,

1 teaspoon crushed dried savoury (or 1 teaspoon chopped fresh savoury),

1/2 teaspoon red pepper,

1 tablespoon vinegar, 2 tablespoons oil, salt

1. Wash beans, put in a saucepan, cover with boiling water. Water should be 4–5 cm over beans. Place lid over saucepan. Cover with a towel and wrap with a woolen blanket. Let soak overnight.

2. Drain beans in a strainer or pour water from saucepan, the lid slightly open. Discard skins, return beans into saucepan and cover with hot water. Water should be 4–5 cm over beans.

3. Cook beans over medium heat. Drain again in a strainer.

4. Combine beans with chopped onions, savoury, red pepper and salt to taste.

5. Blend oil and vinegar and pour over salad.

ROAST PEPPERS SALAD WITH TOMATO SAUCE

INGREDIENT:

1/2 kg peppers, 1 coffee cup oil,

3 tomatoes, 3–4 cloves garlic,

1 tablespoon chopped parsley,

1 tablespoon finely chopped dill, salt

1. Roast and peel peppers (See Roast peppers salad).

2. Sprinkle with salt to taste. Slightly fry in heated oil.

3. Arrange peppers in a deep dish, stems pointing to the edge. Cover with tomato sauce.

4. To make tomato sauce:

Peel and grate tomatoes, put pulp in the oil in which you have fried the peppers, cook over moderate heat.

When sauce is thickened, add crushed garlic cloves and finely chopped parsley and dill.

5. Set peppers aside for 2–3 hours. Serve cold.

FRIED SIRENE

INGREDIENTS:

300 g sirene (white cheese), 2 tablespoons tomato paste,

2 tablespoons flour, 1 egg,

2 tablespoons dry bread crumbs,

1 coffee cup oil

1. Beat egg, blend with tomato paste and flour.

2. Cut cheese in 4 pieces, 1 cm thick. Dip in egg mixture.

3. Toss in bread crumbs until evenly coated. Fry in heated oil on both sides. Serve hot.

20

BAKED SIRENE IN GYUVECHE

INGREDIENTS:

400 g sirene (white cheese), 4 tablespoons butter,
4 tomatoes, 1 onion,
4 eggs, 1 tablespoon oil

1. Peel and grate coarsely tomatoes.
2. Slice thinly onions and fry in oil until golden.
3. Put in each gyuveche (little ceramic bowl) 1 tablespoon butter, equal portions of tomatoes and onions, 100 g cheese and 1 beaten egg.
4. Mix, cover with lid and bake in a moderate oven.
Serve hot.

FRIED BATTER-DIPPED KASHKAVAL

INGREDIENTS:

1/4 kg kashkaval (yellow cheese),
1/2 teaspoon ground black pepper,
1 cup beer, 3 tablespoons flour,
1/3 teaspoon mustard,
2 eggs, separated,
1 1/2 coffee cups oil

1. Cut kashkaval into 6–7 cm long strips, 2 cm wide and 1 1/2 cm thick. Sprinkle with ground black pepper.
2. Prepare batter by mixing well beer, flour, mustard and beaten egg yolks.
3. Beat egg whites until firm. Add gradually to batter, mixing with a fork.
4. Dip cheese pieces in batter to coat and fry in heated oil.
Serve hot with salad at your choice.

FRENCH FRIES WITH SIRENE

INGREDIENTS:

1/2 kg potatoes, 1 1/2 coffee cups oil,
1 tea cup grated sirene (white cheese), salt

1. Peel potatoes, cut lengthwise into edges. Wash and pat dry between two cotton napkins to prevent bubbling when frying.
2. Preheat oil well (lard can also be used). Fry potatoes in portions.
3. Fry potatoes for about 10 minutes. Place on an inverted sieve to drain. Return to hot oil and fry until golden brown.
4. Salt potatoes when they are done. Top with grated cheese and serve.

PANCAKES WITH TOMATO SAUCE

INGREDIENTS:

4 big (or 5 medium) tomatoes,
1 cup fresh milk, 1 egg, 3 tablespoons flour, 1 coffee cup oil,
100 g sirene (white cheese),
1 tablespoon chopped parsley

1. Peel and coarsely grate tomatoes. Simmer, covered, in a small saucepan for 10 minutes. Pass through strainer to remove pips.
2. Set sauce aside to cool. Blend with milk and beaten egg.
Add gradually flour, stirring constantly until batter looks smooth and cream-thick.
3. Fry pancakes in a frying pan, adding some oil for each pancake.
4. Sprinkle each pancake with grated cheese mixed with finely chopped parsley. Fold in two.
Serve hot.

22

SPICY MEAT BALLS

INGREDIENTS:

1/2 kg ground meat, 1/4 kg chicken, 50 g sausage,
2 eggs, 1 slice stale white bread, crust discarded,
1 coffee cup grated kashkaval (yellow cheese), 1/2 teaspoon salt,
1/2 teaspoon ground black pepper, pinch of grated nutmeg,
3 tablespoons flour, 1 coffee cup oil

1. Bone and grind chicken. Mince sausage, beat eggs. Soak bread in water or milk, squeeze dry. Grate cheese.
2. Combine all with minced meat, salt, black pepper, grated nutmeg.
3. Mix well. Shape into walnut-size balls. Roll in flour. Fry in heated oil.
Serve the meatballs warm, with salad at your choice.

CHICKEN SALAD

INGREDIENTS:

1 chicken, 1 celery root, 100 g mayonnaise,
1 teaspoon tomato paste, 1 hard-boiled egg,
vinegar, oil, salt

1. Cook and bone chicken.
2. Peel celery, cut in long thin strips, soak in a mixture of equal portions of oil and vinegar for 1/2 hour.
3. Drain celery. Combine with chicken, cut in small cubes.
4. In a separate small bowl combine mayonnaise with tomato paste.
5. On a big serving plate place celery and chicken, top with mayonnaise, sprinkle salt to taste. Garnish with egg edges.

MUSSELS WITH ONION

INGREDIENTS:
1/4 kg meat of mussels, 1 big onion,
1/2 teaspoon salt, 1/2 teaspoon freshly ground black pepper,
1 tablespoon chopped dill, 1 tablespoon oil,
lemon juice, 10–12 olives

1. Cook mussels for 15 minutes. (Canned cooked mussels can be used too.)
2. Fry lightly mussels in oil or butter if you wish.
3. Combine with finely grated onion, add salt, black pepper, oil and lemon juice to taste.
4. Garnish salad with olives.

FRESH SALTED BONITO SALAD

INGREDIENTS:
1 medium salted bonito, 1 tablespoon lemon juice,
1 tablespoon oil, 1 onion, salt

1. Skin and bone bonito, slice thinly.
2. Arrange slices in a serving plate, slightly covering each other. Sprinkle with lemon juice and oil.
3. Chop finely onion, crush with a little salt.
4. Garnish bonito with onion.

Soups

TARATOR
(COLD YOGURT-CUCUMBER SOUP)

INGREDIENTS:
300–400 g cucumbers, 1/2 kg yogurt,
7–8 walnut kernels, 5–6 cloves garlic, 1 teaspoon vinegar,
1 tablespoon oil, 1/3 cup chopped dill, salt

1. Peel and dice cucumbers.
2. Beat up yogurt using fork or egg-whisk, thin with water, pour over cucumbers.
3. Add chopped walnuts.
4. In a wooden mortar crush garlic, stir in vinegar, add to tarator.
5. Add oil, salt to taste and chopped dill.

MONASTERY WHITE BEANS SOUP

INGREDIENTS:
1 cup white beans, 2 carrots,
1 celery root, 1 parsnip root, 2 parsley roots, 15–20 seed onions,
1 tablespoon finely chopped mint, 1 tablespoon thyme, 1 tablespoon dill,
2–3 tomatoes (fresh or canned), salt

1. Wash beans, soak overnight in cold water with 1 teaspoon salt.
2. In the morning wash beans, drain. Put beans in a saucepan, cover with cold water. Water should be 4–5 cm over beans. Bring to boil. It's better to drain again and to add fresh hot water. Cook beans over low heat for 20 minutes, adding hot water from time to time.
3. Add diced carrots, celery, parsnip and parsley roots, whole seed onions.
4. When beans are almost done, add coarsely grated tomatoes and spices. Sprinkle with salt to taste.
5. If desired, add some vinegar and a chili pepper.

MONASTERY LENTILS SOUP

INGREDIENTS:
1 cup lentils, 1 leek, 2 carrots,
1 small (1/2 big) celery root, 1 tomato, 1 bulb garlic,
1/2 coffee cup oil, 1 sprig dried savoury, 1 teaspoon chopped parsley,
salt, vinegar

1. Wash lentils thoroughly, cover with 1 1/2 liters cold water. Peel and dice carrots and celery, chop leek. Cook lentils over medium heat together with leek, carrots and celery.

2. When lentils are almost done, add oil, non-peeled garlic cloves and savoury.

3. Add coarsely grated tomato 10 minutes before lentils are removed from heat.

4. Season the ready soup with salt and vinegar to taste and sprinkle with chopped parsley.

KURBAN CHORBA
(LAMB SOUP)

INGREDIENTS:
300 g lamb, 2 carrots, 1/2 celery root, 3 tablespoons butter or oil,
1 big (or 2 small) onion, 2 tomatoes (or 1 teaspoon tomato paste),
1 tablespoon flour, 1 potato, 4–5 cloves garlic,
1/2 cup chopped parsley, 1/2 teaspoon ground black pepper, salt

1. Cut lamb in bite-size pieces. Cook in 1 1/2 liters salted water for 15 minutes.

2. Add diced carrots and celery.

3. In a separate pan lightly brown chopped onions in oil or butter. Add to soup together with peeled and coarsely grated tomatoes (or tomato paste diluted with 1 coffee cup warm water).

4. Lightly brown flour in a dry, non-greased pan. Stir in 1 coffee cup lukewarm water. Add to soup. Cook over medium heat for 15 minutes.

5. Add diced potato to soup. When it is done, add finely chopped garlic. Cook for 10 more minutes.

6. Season soup with black pepper, salt to taste and chopped parsley.

VEAL SOUP WITH VEGETABLES

INGREDIENTS:

300 g boned veal (400–500 g with bones), 4–5 medium potatoes,
2 carrots, 4–5 peppers, 5–6 tomatoes,
1 tablespoon flour, 2 tablespoon oil,
1 teaspoon tomato paste, 1/2 teaspoon cumin, 5–6 cloves garlic,
salt, vinegar

1. Cut meat in big pieces. Cook in 1 1/4 liters water.
2. Strain stock. Return meat in stock.
3. Add diced potatoes and finely grated carrots. Cook over medium heat for 10 minutes.
4. Add chopped peppers, stems and seeds discarded, and coarsely grated tomatoes.
5. Lightly brown flour in a non-greased frying pan. Stir in oil and tomato paste diluted with 1 coffee cup warm water.
6. Add mixture to soup, bring to boil. Remove from heat. Season with cumin, vinegar, salt to taste and crushed garlic.

CHICKEN SOUP

INGREDIENTS:

1 chicken (about 600 g), 1 carrot, 1 onion,
2 tablespoons butter, 1 coffee cup crumbled vermicelli,
3 egg yolks, 1/2 teaspoon ground black pepper,
salt, lemon juice

1. Wash chicken. Cover with 1 liter cold water, add salt to taste. Bring to boil. Skim well.
2. Add onion (chopped and lightly browned in butter) and carrot cut in rounds. Cook over medium heat.
3. When chicken is almost done, bone it, cut meat in small pieces and return to stock. Cook for 15 minutes.
4. Add crumbled vermicelli and in 5–6 more minutes – the egg mixture. Prepare egg mixture in the following way: beat up yolks in a separate bowl, pour slowly

several ladles boiling stock over them, stirring all the time to prevent yolks curdling. Remove soup from heat. Add egg mixture. Stir very well.

5. Season soup with black pepper and lemon juice or salt of lemon.

SHKEMBE CHORBA
(TRIPE SOUP)

INGREDIENTS:
1/2 kg veal tripe, 1 coffee cup milk or yogurt,
1 bulb garlic, ground black pepper,
salt, vinegar, red pepper

1. Clean tripe very well, especially folded parts: scrub them with a knife and wash thoroughly. If tripe is not very fresh, soak for some time in water with a little vinegar.

2. In order to preserve tripe's nourishing qualities, put the whole piece in a saucepan with 2 liters boiling water. Cook until tripe is tender (around 3 hours). Add some boiling water if necessary. It takes less (about 1 1/2 hours) if pressure cooker is used.

3. Take it out of the stock, drain and cut in small pieces (scissors can be used). Strain stock. Return cut tripe in it.

4. Add milk or yogurt, stirring all the time, season with salt and pepper and remove from heat.

5. Puree garlic, mix with vinegar. Season soup with black pepper and garlic-vinegar mixture to taste.

Add some chili peppers, roasted and covered generously with oil-vinegar mixture (optional).

DANUBE FISH SOUP

INGREDIENTS:
1/2 kg small fish, heads and tails discarded, or heads and tails of fairly big carps,
2–3 onions, 2–3 peppers, chili peppers (optional),

1 parsley root, piece of celery, 1 sprig of fresh or dried savoury,
2–3 potatoes, 2 tablespoons oil,
2–3 tomatoes (or 2 teaspoons tomato paste, or 2–3 coffee cups tomato juice),
1 tablespoon chopped parsley, 1 tablespoon chopped dill,
1 teaspoon rubbed savoury, 1 teaspoon rubbed dried cow-parsley,
1 teaspoon rubbed dried thyme, salt

This recipe is a variety of the sheath-fish, pike and pike-perch soups cooked in the River Danube region. Other kinds of freshwater fish can also be used.

1. Chop onion, seed and stem peppers, cut in thin rings. If desired, put also some chili peppers split in half. Put all in 1 1/2 liters cold water. Add parsley root, scraped off, together with celery piece, savoury sprig and diced potatoes. Add oil and cook, covered, over medium heat, till vegetables are tender.

2. Strain stock through strainer (not colander) so that stock be clear, pour into another saucepan. Bring to boil, drop pieces of fish (or whole small fish). Skim well and salt to taste. Continue to cook, adding some hot water when necessary.

3. When fish is tender add tomatoes, skinned and coarsely grated (or tomato paste diluted with 1 1/2 coffee cups warm water; tomato juice can also be used). Lower heat and cook for 15 more minutes.

4. Remove saucepan from heat. Add spices: dill, parsley, savoury, cow-parsley and thyme. Fresh cow-parsley has a very strong scent and can suppress all other smells if it is in big quantity. Put all spices at a time and do not stir. Stir only when you ladle the soup in the dishes.

5. Souring agent is very important for soups. Vinegar is not suitable for fish soup. Lemon juice or salt of lemon should be used instead. Black pepper is added to taste.

Freshly baked bread and chilled grape brandy go well with this soup.

Vegetable dishes

CHOMLEK
(VEGETABLE STEW)

INGREDIENTS FOR 5 SERVINGS:
1 kg seed onions, 2 big onions,
1 coffee cup oil, 3–5 big tomatoes (or 1 cup tomato juice),
1 bulb garlic, 1 tablespoon flour,
1 teaspoon red pepper, 1/2 teaspoon ground black pepper,
1 bay leaf, salt, 1 sprig of savoury,
1 coffee cup red wine

1. Chop finely the big onions, lightly brown in oil until golden.
2. Add tomatoes, skinned and finely grated, the peeled seed onions, minced garlic, red and ground black pepper, bay leaf and warm water enough to cover the seed onions. Add wine, salt, sprig of savoury and simmer, covered, until seed onions are tender.
3. Fry flour in a non-greased pan until lightly brown. Stir in 1 coffee cup lukewarm water. Pour over seed onions. Let simmer for 10 more minutes.
This dish will taste much better if cooked in a ceramic casserole.

VEGETABLE KAPAMA

INGREDIENTS FOR 2 SERVINGS:
3 finely chopped onions, 4–5 potatoes, cut in thin slices,
1 chopped parsley root, salt,
1/2 teaspoon ground black pepper, 1 teaspoon tomato paste,
1 tablespoon flour, 1 coffee cup oil, 2 diced carrots, 1 diced piece of celery

1. Bring to boil 1/2 liter water. Drop onions, potatoes, carrots, celery and parsley root.
2. Dilute tomato paste with 1 coffee cup warm water. Fry flour in a dry, non-

greased pan until lightly brown, stir in 1 coffee cup lukewarm water. Add all to dish. Sprinkle with salt and 1/2 teaspoon ground black pepper.

3. Pour in oil, stir very well and let simmer, covered, until water is almost evaporated.

Serve sprinkled with freshly ground black pepper.

PRIEST'S STEW

INGREDIENTS:
800 g seed onions, 1 big onion, 1 leek,
4 tablespoons oil, 1 tablespoon flour, 5–6 cloves garlic, 1 bay leaf,
10–12 black peppercorns, salt,
1 teaspoon red pepper, 2 teaspoons tomato paste

1. Chop onion and leek, fry lightly in oil.
2. Lightly brown flour in a dry, non-greased pan, stir in 1 coffee cup lukewarm water. Add to onion-leek mixture.
3. Drop seed onions in boiling water. Cook for several minutes. Drain. Drop them in fresh boiling water and cook until tender. Drain well. Combine with finely chopped garlic, bay leaf, black peppercorns, salt, red pepper and tomato paste, diluted with 1 1/2 coffee cups warm water.
4. Add to onion-flour mixture. Pour in warm water enough to cover seed onions. Let simmer for 45 minutes. Serve immediately.

WHITE BEANS STEW

INGREDIENTS:
2 cups white beans, 2–3 small onions, 1 pepper (fresh or dry),
1 carrot, 1 piece of celery,
2 parsley roots, 1 tablespoon dried cow-parsley,
1 tablespoon dried mint, 1 sprig of savoury (fresh or dried),
1 big onion, 3 tablespoons oil,
1 teaspoon red pepper, 2–3 tomatoes (or 1 tablespoon tomato paste),
1 tablespoon chopped fresh mint, 1 tablespoon chopped fresh cow-parsley, salt

1. Wash beans. Cover with cold water, add 1 teaspoon salt and soak overnight.

2. Wash beans again. Cover with cold water. Cook over medium heat. If desired, cook beans for several minutes, drain and cover with fresh boiling water, and then continue to cook for 20 more minutes.

3. Add the peeled whole small onions, fresh or dried pepper (you can put one fresh and one dried pepper). If you like spicy food you can drop one chili pepper, fresh or dried, to boil for about 10 minutes with the beans. Add some water, if necessary. It must be hot, so that cooking does not stop.

4. Remove small onions when done, using a slotted spoon, puree them with wooden spoon and return to saucepan. If you do not have small onions, use 1 big onion, finely chopped, instead. In this case there is no need to puree it.

5. Add peeled and sliced carrot and diced celery.

6. Salt to taste. Peel and wash parsley roots. Drop in saucepan together with dried mint, dried cow-parsley and savoury (fresh or dried, or both)

7. In another saucepan slightly fry in oil 1 finely chopped onion.

8. Remove saucepan from heat, stir in red pepper, add several tablespoons bean stock, stir well with wooden spoon, return saucepan on heat . Add skinned and coarsely grated tomatoes or tomato paste diluted with 2 coffee cups of bean stock.

9. Using a slotted spoon take out from the first saucepan parsley roots, celery, carrots and peppers. Transfer beans to the second saucepan.

10. Cook for 20 minutes over low heat. Add finely chopped fresh mint.

11. Sprinkle with chopped fresh cow-parsley and serve.

LENTILS PLAKIA

INGREDIENTS:
1/4 kg lentils, 1 bulb garlic, 2 tablespoons oil,
1 tablespoon chopped fresh dill, salt, vinegar

1. Soak lentils in cold water for 4–5 hours. Cook in a saucepan until the beans are fully done and the dish becomes thicker.

2. Twenty minutes after lentils have started boiling, add non-peeled cloves garlic. Pour in oil.

3. At the end of cooking sprinkle with chopped dill, season with salt and vinegar to taste.

IMAM BAYELDI
(AUBERGINES STUFFED WITH VEGETABLES)

INGREDIENTS:
4 big aubergines (or 6 small ones), 4 carrots,
4 onions, 4 peppers, 5 tomatoes, 1/2 celery root,
5–6 cloves garlic, 1/2 bunch chopped parsley,
2 tablespoons dry bread crumbs, 1 coffee cup oil, salt

1. Cut stems of aubergines. Peel each in 2–3 centimeter-wide strips, zebra-like, alternating with 2 centimeter-wide non-peeled strips. Sprinkle peeled places with salt. Place aubergines in a tilted pan for 1 hour, allowing bitter juices to run out. Wash aubergines and pat dry. Make deep slits in the skinned strips.

2. Slightly fry in oil aubergines on all sides. Remove from pan. Set aside in a plate in a warm place on the stove.

3. In the same oil lightly brown finely chopped onion. Add finely grated carrots, finely chopped peppers, 4 tomatoes, skinned and coarsely grated; very finely minced garlic, finely chopped parsley and diced celery.

4. Pour in some hot water and let simmer, uncovered until water is evaporated.

5. Let mixture cool slightly. Stuff slits in the aubergines with it. Place aubergines in a greased ceramic casserole or in a greased baking pan.

6. Place a tomato slice on each aubergine. Sprinkle each one with 1/2 table-spoon each dry bread crumbs and chopped parsley.

7. Pour hot water in baking pan enough to cover 2/3 of aubergines. Bake in a moderate oven.

Serve cold.

SARMI (STUFFED VINE LEAVES)

INGREDIENTS:
20 vine leaves, 2–3 onions, 3 tablespoons oil,
1 coffee cup rice, salt, 1 teaspoon red pepper,
1/2 teaspoon ground black pepper, 1/2 teaspoon crushed dried savoury,
2–3 eggs, 1 cup yogurt

1. Scald vine leaves in boiling water. If canned leaves are used, just soak them in lukewarm water for 1/2 hour.

2. Chop finely onion. Lightly brown in oil, adding 1 coffee cup warm water and cook until tender.

3. Wash and dry rice. Add to onion.

4. Season with salt, savoury, red and black pepper.

5. Simmer over low heat until rice is done, adding a little hot water now and then.

6. Put 1 tablespoon of mixture in the middle of each leaf and fold carefully.

7. Place an inverted plate on the bottom of a saucepan. Arrange tightly the folded leaves (sarmi). Cover with another inverted plate.

8. Cover with hot water enough to cover the sarmi. Let simmer over low heat.

9. Beat up eggs. Blend with yogurt. Pour mixture over dish and cook for 10 more minutes.

CABBAGE LEAVES (SARMI)
STUFFED WITH WHITE BEANS

INGREDIENTS:
12 sour cabbage leaves,
1 1/2 cups cooked, drained white beans, stock reserved,
2 onions, 1 coffee cup rice,
1 teaspoon red pepper, 4–5 dry red peppers,
50 g salted bacon,
1/2 teaspoon ground black pepper, salt

1. Wash rice and cook in 3 coffee cups water until done. Drain.

2. Combine with cooked drained beans, chopped onion, black and red pepper. Sprinkle with salt to taste, mix well.

3. Put some of the mixture in the middle of each cabbage leaf and wrap carefully. The stems inside each leaf should be cut so that it rolls up better round the stuffing. Put several cabbage leaves on the bottom of a saucepan. Arrange sarmi on them. Put pieces of dry peppers between them.

4. Cover sarmi with equal portions of sour cabbage juice and stock in which you have cooked the beans. The liquid should be 2–3 cm below the surface of the dish.

5. Top sarmi with thinly sliced bacon. Cover with an inverted plate. If you do not like bacon, blend oil with some red pepper and pour over sarmi.

6. Cook over low heat.

PEPPERS STUFFED WITH VEGETABLES

INGREDIENTS:

12 big bell peppers, 2 carrots, 1/2 celery, 2 onions,
3 tablespoons oil, 4–5 potatoes, 4 tomatoes,
6–7 cloves garlic, 1 coffee cup crumbled sirene (white cheese),
1 tablespoon chopped parsley, 2 tablespoons butter,
2 eggs, 1 cup milk, salt

1. Cut off tops of peppers, discard seeds and sprinkle with a little salt.
2. Dice carrots and celery, chop onion. Lightly brown in oil, add 1 coffee cup warm water and cook until soft.
3. Add diced potatoes, 2 tomatoes, skinned and coarsely grated, very finely chopped garlic, crumbled cheese and chopped parsley.
4. Mix well and fill peppers. Place in a greased baking pan. Grate coarsely remaining tomatoes. Spoon among peppers.
5. Pour in warm water to cover 2/3 of the height of peppers. Put a dot of butter on each pepper.
6. Bake in a moderate oven.
7. Beat up eggs, blend with milk. Pour over peppers. Bake for 10 more minutes.

GREEN ZUCCHINI STUFFED
WITH SIRENE

INGREDIENTS:

8 zucchini, equal in length, 2 onions,
2 coffee cups oil, 1 tablespoon flour,
1 cup grated sirene (white cheese), 3 eggs,
1 tablespoon chopped parsley, 1 cup milk

1. Peel zucchini and scrape out most of the pulp, using a sharp knife.
2. Chop onion. Stew in 3 tablespoons oil and some water.
3. Lightly brown flour in a non-greased pan. Add to stewed onion and fry lightly. Stir in 1 coffee cup warm water.
4. Beat up 2 eggs. Combine with crumbled cheese and chopped parsley. Add to onion mixture and stir well.

5. Fill zucchini with this mixture and place in a greased baking pan.

6. Beat up remaining egg, blend with milk. Add zucchini pulp. Pour over zucchini in the baking pan.

7. Bake in a moderate oven for 20 minutes. Pour in remaining oil. Bake 10 more minutes.

GARDENER'S STUFFED AUBERGINES

INGREDIENTS:

4 medium aubergines, 3 coffee cups oil,
3–4 potatoes, 2 carrots, piece of celery,
2 onions, 4–5 tomatoes, 6–7 cloves garlic,
2 coffee cups crumbled sirene (white cheese),
2 tablespoons chopped parsley,
2–3 eggs, 1 cup milk, salt

1. Choose dark glossy aubergines. Cut tops off. Using a teaspoon, scoop out most of pulp. Salt both scooped aubergines and pulp. Place aubergines in a tilted baking pan for 1 hour, to allow bitter juices run out.

2. Wash aubegines and pat dry. Fry lightly in 1 coffee cup heated oil.

3. Peel potatoes, carrots and celery. Cook them, then dice.

4. Fry finely chopped onion in 1 coffee cup oil until golden. Combine with cooked vegetables, aubergine pulp, tomatoes (skinned and coarsely grated), garlic (crushed with a little salt).

5. In 5–6 minutes remove saucepan from heat, add crumbled cheese and chopped parsley. Salt to taste. Stir.

6. Stuff aubergines with the mixture. Place in a baking pan, cover with remaining oil and warm water, enough to cover 2/3 of aubergines. Tomato juice can be used instead of water.

7. Bake in a moderate oven for 40 minutes. When the aubergines are ready, pour over a mixture made of eggs, beaten up and blended with milk. Bake 10 more minutes.

POTATO BALLS WITH SIRENE

INGREDIENTS FOR 5 SERVINGS:

1 kg potatoes, 2 eggs, 1 onion,
1 cup grated sirene (white cheese), 2 tablespoons chopped parsley, salt,
1/2 teaspoon ground black pepper,
2 tablespoons flour, 1 coffee cup oil, 1 tablespoon chopped dill,
3–4 cloves garlic, crushed with a little salt,
1/2 kg yogurt

1. Boil potatoes, peel while still warm. Allow to cool and grate coarsely.
2. Beat up eggs, chop onion, grate cheese, chop parsley. Combine all with grated potatoes. Season with salt and black pepper.
3. Stir well and shape into balls. Roll in flour and fry in heated oil.
4. Serve with yogurt mixed with chopped dill and crushed garlic.

BAKED NEW POTATOES

INGREDIENTS:

600 g new potatoes, 2 onions (or 2 cups chopped green onions),
1 coffee cup oil, 1 tablespoon flour,
1 teaspoon tomato paste (or 1 tomato: fresh or canned),
2 tablespoons butter, salt

1. Skin potatoes, wash and cut in big cubes. Boil in a small quantity of water.
2. In another pan lightly brown in oil finely chopped onion.
3. Fry flour in a dry, non-greased pan until lightly brown, stir in 1 coffee cup lukewarm water. Mix with tomato paste (or with the tomato, skinned and grated). Combine with lightly browned onion.
4. Combine in one pan potatoes and onion mixture, season, mix well.
5. Pour mixture into a greased baking pan. Dot with butter.
6. Bake in a moderate oven until potato crust becomes golden-brown.

AUBERGINES WITH TOMATOES

INGREDIENTS:
1/2 kg aubergines, 2 coffee cups oil,
1 bunch green onions (or 1 big onion), 3 medium tomatoes,
2 eggs, 1 coffee cup grated kashkaval (yellow cheese),
1 tablespoon cold butter, 3 tablespoons flour,
salt, 1 coffee cup milk

1. Peel and slice aubergines. Salt and place in a tilted pan for 1 hour to allow bitter juices run out.

2. Wash aubergines and pat dry. Roll in flour and fry on both sides in 1 coffee cup oil.

3. In another pan lightly brown onion in remaining oil.

4. Arrange fried aubergines in a baking pan. Cover with lightly browned onion.

5. Top onion with sliced tomatoes.

6. Beat up eggs, blend with milk. Pour over aubergines.

7. Sprinkle with grated kashkaval, dot with butter and bake in a moderate oven for 30–40 minutes or until aubergines are soft.

VEGETABLE GYUVECH
(BAKED MIXED VEGETABLES)

INGREDIENTS:
1 coffee cup oil, 2 onions, 1 zucchini, 1 aubergine,
1 coffee cup green peas (fresh or canned),
1 cup green beans, cut in small pieces (fresh or canned),
3 peppers, 4 potatoes, 1 piece cabbage,
1 cup fresh okra, stems removed,
1 teaspoon red pepper, 3 tomatoes, 3 eggs,
2 tablespoons chopped parsley, salt

A ceramic casserole and a saucepan to lightly brown vegetables will be needed.

1. Cut onion in long, thin strips. Lightly brown in 3 tablespoons oil in saucepan, transfer to casserole.

2. Peel and dice aubergine, salt and set aside for some time to allow bitter juice run out. Wash. Dice zucchini, combine with aubergine. Lightly brown in saucepan until tender. Transfer to casserole.

3. Lightly brown green peas and green beans in oil and some water in sauce-

pan. Transfer to casserole.

4. Cut peppers in rings, dice potatoes. Cut cabbage in long thin strips. Lightly brown all in saucepan and transfer to casserole. Lightly brown okra in the same way and transfer to casserole. Add some oil when necessary while you lightly brown vegetables. Salt mixture in casserole. Sprinkle with red pepper.

5. Place casserole in cold oven because otherwise it will break. Bake gyuvech slowly in oven set at low for about 2 hours.

6. When ready, top with sliced tomatoes and cover with mixture made of beaten eggs combined with chopped parsley.

7. Turn off oven and leave gyuvech in it for 10 more minutes or until eggs are set.

The ceramic casserole can be substituted for a fireproof glass pan or a baking pan.

KACHAMAK (HOMINY)

INGREDIENTS:
1 1/2 cups maize flour (or maize semolina), 3 1/2 cups water,
1 teaspoon salt, 1 teaspoon red pepper,
1 cup crumbled sirene (white cheese), 1/2 coffee cup oil

1. Bring water to boil, add salt. Start adding flour very slowly, stirring all the time with a wooden spoon.

2. Continue to cook stirring all the time until kachamak starts to come off the sides and bottom of saucepan. Transfer into a baking pan.

3. Heat oil in a small frying pan, fry cheese for a short time, stir in red pepper.

4. Spread cheese over kachamak in the baking pan. Using a fork, pierce kachamak in several places, 2–3 cm apart.

PANAGYURSKI EGGS ON YOGURT

INGREDIENTS:
8 eggs, 1/2 kg yogurt,
120 g grated sirene (white cheese),
100 g melted butter, 1 teaspoon red pepper, 1 tablespoon vinegar, salt

1. In a saucepan boil 2 cups water, pour in vinegar. Break eggs one by one in a plate. Transfer carefully to saucepan, trying not to break yolks. Cover saucepan

and cook over low heat until eggs are done.

2. Combine yogurt with grated cheese and divide in 4 individual plates.

3. Using a slotted spoon, take eggs out of the water. Put 2 in each plate.

4. Sprinkle with red pepper and salt. Pour melted butter over eggs.

KAIGANA (OMELET BAKED IN OVEN)

INGREDIENTS:

4 eggs, 1 coffee cup flour, 2 tablespoons butter,
2–3 tablespoons grated kashkaval (yellow cheese) or dry sirene (white cheese),
honey, jam, marmalade, sugar

1. Beat up eggs.

2. Stir in flour, enough to make thick gruel. Salt to taste.

3. Pour mixture into a baking pan, greased with 1 tablespoon butter. Dot with cold butter (1 tablespoon).

4. Bake in a moderate oven.

5. When ready, cut in squares and garnish with grated sirene or grated kashkaval, or with honey, marmalade, jam, sugar.

MOUSSAKA WITH MUSHROOMS

INGREDIENTS:

800 g mushrooms, 1 coffee cup oil, 2 onions, 2 tomatoes,
5 potatoes, 1 teaspoon flour,
2 coffee cups yogurt, salt

For best result use edible boletus.

1. Heat oil and lightly brown finely chopped onion.

2. Clean mushrooms and chop finely. Add to onion and lightly brown, stirring with wooden spoon for 10 minutes.

3. Add coarsely grated tomatoes (or 1 teaspoon tomato paste diluted with 1 coffee cup warm water) to onion-mushroom mixture.

4. Salt and let simmer.

5. In a separate saucepan boil salted water, cook peeled and sliced potatoes. Reserve stock.

6. Drain and arrange half of potatoes in a greased baking pan. Cover with half of mushroom mixture.

7. Arrange second half of potatoes. Cover with remaining mushroom mixture.

8. Pour over oil in which you have lightly browned mushrooms. Add stock in which you have cooked potatoes, enough to cover 2/3 of arranged products.

9. Bake in a moderate oven.

10. When the dish is ready, beat up eggs, blend well with flour and yogurt. Pour over moussaka and bake for another 10 minutes.

KATMI (YEAST PANCAKES) WITH MUSHROOMS

INGREDIENTS:

for stuffing – 200 g mushrooms (fresh or canned),
1 onion, 3 tablespoons butter, 1/2 teaspoon ground black pepper;

for pancakes – 1/2 kg flour, yeast the size of a matchbox,
1 teaspoon salt, 1 teaspoon sugar;

bacon, oil

1. Chop finely onion. Lightly brown in 2 tablespoons butter (or oil).

2. Clean, wash and chop mushrooms. Add to onion. Simmer, covered, for 10 minutes. Season with salt and freshly ground black pepper.

3. Combine yeast with salt, sugar, a little flour and warm water enough to make thin gruel. Let stand in a warm place until the surface is frothy.

4. Add water and flour in portions, stirring all the time. Batter should look like a thin gruel.

5. Let stand in a warm place for 1/2 hour.

6. To fry pancakes use a frying pan, preheated and greased with a piece of bacon or a little oil.

7. Pour a ladle of mixture into the heated greased frying pan and fry at moderate heat. Turn and fry the other side of pancake.

8. Put some of the mushroom mixture on each pancake and make a roll. Arrange rolls in a greased with the remaining butter pan. Bake in a moderate oven.

The ingredients are enough to make around 20 katmi.

Meat dishes

LAMB STEW WITH GREEN ONIONS

INGREDIENTS FOR 6 SERVINGS:
1 kg lamb from the breast, 1 coffee cup oil, 3 bunches green onions,
3 tablespoons chopped parsley, 3 tablespoons chopped fresh mint,
1 teaspoon red pepper, 5–6 black peppercorns,
2 tablespoons melted butter,
1/2 teaspoon salt of lemon, salt

1. Cut meat into bite-size pieces. Lightly brown in oil with chopped onions until onions are soft.
2. Add chopped parsley and mint, black pepper, sprinkle with red pepper. Pour in 1 cup lukewarm water, salt. Stir well, add melted butter and simmer until water is totally evaporated.
3. At the end add salt of lemon diluted with 2 tablespoons lukewarm water.

LAMB SARMA-KEBAP

INGREDIENTS FOR 6 SERVINGS:
1 kg lamb, 1 mesentery, 1 coffee cup melted butter (or oil),
1 bunch green onions, 3 tablespoons chopped parsley,
3 tablespoons chopped fresh mint,
1 teaspoon red pepper, 1/2 teaspoon ground black pepper,
1 cup yogurt, 2–3 eggs, salt

1. Wash thoroughly lamb mesentery, soak in cold water for 1 hour. Cut in 10–cm squares.
2. Cut up lamb in small pieces. Heat 2–3 tablespoons butter and lightly brown meat.
3. Chop onions in 2–cm pieces. Add to meat together with 2 tablespoons chopped parsley, the chopped mint, red pepper and ground black pepper. Sprinkle

with salt, stir well and simmer, covered, for only 5 minutes.

4. Put 1–2 tablespoons of mixture in the middle of each mesentery square and wrap carefully sarmi. Place in a greased baking pan .

5. Pour in 1 cup of warm water and bake in a moderate oven.

6. Beat up eggs, blend with yogurt, add 1 tablespoon chopped parsley. Cover sarmi with mixture and bake for several more minutes or until eggs are set.

LAMB STEWED WITH NEW POTATOES

INGREDIENTS:
800 g lamb, 1/2 kg new potatoes,
4 tablespoons oil (or melted butter), 1 onion, 1 tablespoon flour,
1 teaspoon tomato paste, 1 teaspoon red pepper,
1/2 teaspoon ground black pepper,
2 tablespoons chopped parsley, salt

1. Cut up meat in bite-size pieces. Fry in oil on all sides.

2. Using a slotted spoon, take out meat. Transfer to another saucepan and keep in a warm place. Reserve oil.

3. Chop onion. Fry flour in a non-greased pan, stir in 1 coffee cup lukewarm water. Combine with onion and fry in oil.

4. Add tomato paste diluted with 1 coffee cup warm water. Season with salt to taste and red pepper. Pour in 1 cup of warm water and cook, covered, at moderate heat.

5. In 15 minutes add fried meat and peeled and washed potatoes. Slice bigger ones and leave smaller ones whole.

6. Simmer at low heat until meat is tender and potatoes are fully cooked.

7. Serve sprinkled with chopped parsley.

LAMB KAPAMA

INGREDIENTS: 600 g lamb, 3 tablespoons melted butter,
2 bunches green onions, 1 bunch parsley, 1 bunch fresh mint,
1 tablespoon flour, salt

1. Cut meat in bite-size pieces. Lightly brown in melted butter in a saucepan over medium heat, covered.

2. Salt meat, cover with chopped onions cut in 2–cm pieces.

3. Top onions with finely chopped parsley, and sprinkle mint over parsley.

4. Fry slightly flour in a pan. Stir in 1 coffee cup warm water. Pour mixture in saucepan.

5. Simmer, covered, over medium heat, until meat is tender. Add some warm water, if necessary.

6. Serve kapama with finely chopped parsley and fresh mint.

LAMB WITH SPICY SAUCE

INGREDIENTS FOR 6 SERVINGS:

1 kg lamb, 1/2 kg yogurt, 7 tablespoons oil,
3 tablespoons flour, 1/2 teaspoon ground black pepper, 5 eggs,
1 teaspoon red pepper, salt

1. Bone meat and cut in bite-size pieces. Cook in salted water.

2. Take meat out of saucepan and strain stock.

3. In a big saucepan put yogurt, 3 tablespoons oil, flour mixture (first fry flour in a non-greased pan until golden and stir in 2 coffee cups lukewarm water) and ground black pepper.

4. Add eggs one by one, stirring well with an wooden spoon after each.

5. Cook over low heat for 5–6 minutes, stirring now and then with a wooden spoon.

6. Add some stock, enough to make a moderately thick sauce.

7. Continue to cook, increase heat. When mixture comes to boil, remove saucepan from heat. Keep on stirring until sauce is cool – then add cooked lamb.

8. In a separate pan fry slightly red pepper in 4 tablespoons oil. Pour over dish before serving.

GRANDMOTHER'S LAMB GYUVECH

INGREDIENTS FOR 6 SERVINGS:

1 kg lamb internal parts (hearts, kidneys, and others) or 1 kg breast, cutlets and tails,
1 coffee cup melted butter, 1 tablespoon tomato paste,
1 teaspoon red pepper, 3 bunches green onions,
1 tablespoon ground black pepper,
1 tablespoon chopped fresh mint, 3–4 tomatoes, salt

1. Cut parts (or breast, cutlets and tails) in bite-size pieces, fry slightly in butter.
2. Add tomato paste (diluted with 1 1/2 coffee cups warm water), red pepper, green onions cut in 2 cm pieces.
3. Cover with water and cook over medium heat for 15 minutes.
4. Season with salt to taste, ground black pepper and finely chopped mint.
5. Mix well and transfer to a preheated ceramic casserole (or baking pan).
6. Bake in a moderate oven until parts (or meat) are half-cooked. Add sliced tomatoes.
7. Continue to bake in a moderate oven until liquid is fully absorbed.

STUFFED LAMB LEG

INGREDIENTS FOR 8 SERVINGS:

1 lamb leg, 200 g ground lamb, 100 g smoked or salted bacon,
3 eggs, 1 teaspoon ground black pepper,
1 coffee cup oil, 1 1/2 cups tomato juice, salt

1. Discard carefully bone from leg so that you get a deep slit in the meat.
2. Combine ground lamb, diced bacon, beaten eggs, ground black pepper and salt to taste.
3. Mix well, spoon mixture in slit and sew up opening with white thread.
4. Heat oil. Fry leg on all sides. Place in a baking pan. Pour equal portions of warm water and tomato juice over leg. The liquid should cover 2/3 of meat.
5. Bake in a moderate oven.

CHEVERME
(LAMB BARBECUE)

This is an ancient way to cook lamb in the open. Today it is served in some specialized restaurants.

1. Remove internal parts, wash lamb very well, pat dry, sprinkle with salt on all sides, sew up stomach opening with white thread.

2. Skewer lamb on a good wooden spit, 2 m long. (In old times they also used long metal spits).

3. Roast lamb over live coals for 3–4 hours, turning it all the time. Turn it faster in the beginning, until lamb is evenly browned on all sides. Slow down turning. Using a long stick, rub lamb from time to time with a piece of cotton material soaked in tallow from the lamb mesentery, or in oil.

4. The lamb is ready when, if pierced with a sharp knife, clear juices run out (not blood).

Cooking tips: put ends of spit with the skewered lamb on two big wooden forks fixed into the ground. Lamb should be about 40 cm over the live coals. If flames appear during roasting, immediately put them out, sprinkling with water. For this purpose you should have a container with water near the fire.

MUTTON SHISH-KEBAP

INGREDIENTS FOR 3 SERVINGS:

600 g boned tender, lean mutton,
3 onions, cut in large pieces,
2-3 green or red peppers, cut into pieces, some seed onions,
1 teaspoon salt, 1 teaspoon ground black pepper,
1 teaspoon ground cumin

1. Cut meat into 2 cm cubes and place in a saucepan.
2. In a separate saucepan cook onion in 2 tea cups water.
3. When onion is tender, strain water. Let cool. Pour over meat.

4. Add salt, ground black pepper and cumin. Cover and let in a cool place overnight.

5. Drain meat, pat dry and skewer on metal skewers. Put pepper pieces and seed onions (or pieces of onion, if desired), alternating with meat.

6. Roast skewers over live coals. If flames appear, put them out with water to avoid blackening of meat.

7. Skewers can also be placed in a baking pan and baked in oven, pouring some marinade in pan.

Serve hot.

MUTTON IN GYUVECHE

INGREDIENTS:

1 kg fat mutton, 6 tomatoes, 1 coffee cup oil,
3 onions, 1/4 kg peppers, seeds and stems discarded,
1 kg potatoes, peeled and cut in edges,
salt, 1 teaspoon red pepper,
1 teaspoon ground black pepper, 6 chili peppers

1. Wash meat, pat dry, cut in small pieces. Cook in some water until tender.

2. Divide meat in 6 individual ceramic bowls (gyuveche). Place 1 sliced tomato over meat in each one.

3. In a saucepan stew finely chopped onion in oil and some water. Divide in the individual dishes. In the same oil lightly brown sliced peppers, transfer to bowls. Repeat the same with potatoes.

4. In a small bowl mix salt, red pepper, ground black pepper. Stir in 1 coffee cup lukewarm water. Pour evenly into bowls.

5. Put 1 chili pepper in each bowl (optional).

6. Pour some warm water in each bowl. It should be 2–3 cm below the surface of products. In the beginning bake in a hot oven but when liquid comes to boil, reduce heat.

7. Bake in a slow oven until liquid is fully evaporated.

Serve hot.

VEAL WITH PLUMS

INGREDIENTS: 1 kg veal from the shoulder, 3 tablespoons oil, 1 onion,
1 teaspoon red pepper, 1/2 kg dried plums,
1 teaspoon tomato paste, pinch of cinnamon,
2 tablespoons butter, 1 full tablespoon flour, salt

1. Fry slightly meat in oil.
2. Add chopped onion and lightly brown.
3. Season with red pepper and salt to taste. Pour in some warm water to cover meat. Cook over medium heat until meat is tender.
4. Soak dried plums for 1 hour in warm water, pit. Add to meat and continue to cook for 10 more minutes.
5. Dilute tomato paste with 1 coffee cup warm water. Add to meat. Sprinkle with cinnamon and continue to cook until meat is ready.
6. Fry flour in butter and add to meat.
7. If desired, caramelize 1–2 tablespoons sugar and add to meat before flour.

VEAL STEWED IN WINE

INGREDIENTS:
600 – 700 g boned veal, 2 coffee cups melted butter (or oil),
1 tablespoon flour, 1 cup red wine, 3 onions, finely chopped,
1 teaspoon tomato paste, 1 teaspoon red pepper,
10 –12 black peppercorns, 1 bay leaf, salt

1. Cut meat in cubes and lightly brown in 1 coffee cup butter or oil.
2. Fry flour in a dry, non-greased frying pan until lightly brown. Stir in 1 coffee cup lukewarm water. Add to meat. Stir well. Add wine and cook over low heat, covered, until meat is half-done.
3. In a separate saucepan lightly brown chopped onion in 1 coffee cup butter or oil.
4. Dilute tomato paste with 1 coffee cup warm water. Add to onion. Sprinkle with red pepper. Immediately pour over 1 coffee cup warm water. Stir well. Add black pepper and bay leaf.

5. Bring mixture to boil. Pour over meat.

6. Salt to taste and simmer, covered, until meat is ready and liquid is fully absorbed.

SPICY VEAL KAVARMA
WITH MUSHROOMS

INGREDIENTS:

600 – 700 g boned veal,

1 coffee cup oil, 1 onion, 1/2 kg mushrooms (fresh or canned),

1 teaspoon red pepper, 1/2 teaspoon ground black pepper,

3 tablespoons chopped fresh mint, 3 tablespoons chopped parsley,

pinch of savoury, salt

1. Cut meat in cubes. Cook in lightly salted water.

2. Take meat out, using a slotted spoon and lightly brown in oil in a separate saucepan. Reserve stock.

3. Add chopped onion. Stir. Continue to fry at low heat for 10 minutes.

4. Clean mushrooms, wash and cut into small pieces. Add to meat. Sprinkle with red pepper, pour in 1 cup of stock and cook, covered, over medium heat until meat is done.

5. Sprinkle with ground black pepper, finely chopped fresh mint, parsley and savoury.

Serve hot.

GARDENER'S VEAL GYUVECH
(BAKED VEAL WITH VEGETABLES)

INGREDIENTS:

600 – 700 veal, 1 1/2 coffee cups melted butter (or oil),

3 finely chopped onions,

1 teaspoon red pepper, 1/2 teaspoon ground black pepper, 6–7 peppers,

1 aubergine, 1 cup okra, 3–4 tomatoes, salt

1. Cut veal in pieces. Salt. In a saucepan lightly brown meat and chopped onion in 1/2 coffee cup butter (or oil).

2. When onion is transparent, add red and black pepper, salt to taste. Stir and immediately transfer to a preheated ceramic casserole or a baking pan.

3. Pour remaining butter (or oil) in saucepan and lightly brown, one at a time, peppers, cut in rings, diced aubergine and okra, stems removed. (Aubergine should be peeled, salted and left aside for 1 hour in a tilted pan to allow bitter juices run out). Transfer to casserole.

4. Pour remaining butter (or oil) in the casserole (or baking pan). It will be warm. Place it in cold oven.

5. Start baking over medium heat for 20 minutes, then set oven at low. The dish is ready when the liquid is fully evaporated.

6. Cover dish with sliced tomatoes and bake for 10 more minutes.

KNUCKLE OF VEAL BAKED IN OVEN

INGREDIENTS:

1 knuckle of veal, 1 teaspoon ground black pepper,
6–7 cloves crushed garlic, 1 teaspoon crushed savoury,
1 coffee cup oil, 1 cup red wine, salt

1. Cook knuckle until it becomes easy to remove meat from bones. Let cool.

2. Remove bone and pound meat like a steak, but very lightly.

3. Sprinkle with salt to taste, ground black pepper and rubbed savoury. Cover with a thin layer of crushed garlic.

4. Roll meat. Tie with white thread or stick in metal skewers on each side. Place roll in a baking pan.

5. Pour in oil, 1 cup warm water and 1 cup red wine.

6. Bake meat in a moderate oven, basting from time to time with some stock from pan.

7. Serve meat cut up in pieces, covered with sauce.

Garnish with boiled potatoes (optional).

VEAL VRETENO (STUFFED VEAL)

INGREDIENTS FOR 6 SERVINGS:
1 kg veal tenderloin, 1 teaspoon ground black pepper,
10–12 black peppercorns, 3 coffee cups oil, 3 onions,
100 g mushrooms (fresh or canned), 6 hard-boiled eggs,
1 coffee cup grated kashkaval (yellow cheese),
2 tablespoons chopped parsley, 2 tablespoons butter,
1 coffee cup flour, salt

1. Cut meat in fillets. Pound with a pestle. Sprinkle with salt and ground black pepper.
2. Prepare stuffing: Chop onion and fresh mushrooms, cleaned and washed (canned ones can be used instead). Lightly brown in 1 coffee cup oil. Add diced eggs, grated kashkaval, chopped parsley, black pepper, crushed in a mortar, and salt to taste.
3. Put some stuffing on each fillet, dot with butter (soft but cold).
4. Roll fillets and fix ends with 2 metal skewers (or tooth-picks) at each end.
5. Roll in flour and deep–fry in 2 coffee cups oil.
6. Serve with boiled vegetables and/or French fries.

PORK WITH SOUR CABBAGE

INGREDIENTS: 600–700 g pork, 2 onions,
1 tablespoon lard (or oil), 1 medium sour cabbage,
2 coffee cups white wine, 1 celery leaf,
2 bay leaves, 10–12 black peppercorns

1. Lightly brown in oil finely chopped onion.
2. Cut cabbage in thin strips. Wash with cold water, squeeze dry and combine with onion.
3. Cut meat in small pieces. Combine with cabbage and onion. Add black pepper, chopped celery leaf and bay leaves.
4. Pour wine and warm water enough to cover 2/3 of products.
5. Cook, covered, over low heat, until cabbage and meat are done.

6. Transfer mixture to a baking pan and bake for 1/2 hour in a moderate oven. Serve with boiled potatoes.

PORK LEG STEWED WITH GARLIC

INGREDIENTS FOR 6 SERVINGS:
1 kg pork from the leg,
2 onions, 3 parsley roots, 3 bay leaves, 50 g bacon, 1 bulb garlic,
1/2 celery, salt

1. Using a sharp knife make slits in meat. Fill with pieces of bacon, cloves garlic and bay leaf pieces.
2. Rub meat with salt. Place it in a big saucepan, together with whole onions, sliced celery, parsley roots and 2 bay leaves.
3. Cover with warm water and cook, covered, until meat is done.
4. Take it out and slice thinly.
Serve cold, garnished with pickles.

PORK KAVARMA
(SPICY STEWED PORK)

INGREDIENTS FOR 6 SERVINGS:
1 kg boned pork, 3 tablespoons lard (or oil),
10–12 black peppercorns, 1 teaspoon crushed savoury,
1/2 cup red wine, salt

1. Cut meat into bite-size pieces. Lightly brown for 5–6 minutes in heated fat, stirring with wooden spoon.
2. Cover with warm water and simmer, covered. At the tenth minute add finely chopped onion, black pepper and savoury.
3. Salt to taste, pour in wine and simmer until meat is completely done.
4. Transfer mixture to a baking pan and bake for 20 minutes (optional).

PORK KAPAMA
(PORK BAKED IN A CERAMIC CASSEROLE)

INGREDIENTS FOR 6 SERVINGS:
1 kg pork, 6 tablespoons lard (or oil),
2 onions, 1 carrot, 1/2 celery, 4–5 dry red peppers,
2–3 tomatoes (fresh or canned), 1 teaspoon red pepper,
1 teaspoon ground black pepper, 1 tablespoon chopped parsley, salt

Use a big ceramic casserole with a lid or fireproof dish, also with a lid. If the dish has no lid, cover it with cooking foil. For best results use breast, but ribs can also be used.

1. Cut up meat in large pieces. Boil in salted water, stirring with wooden spoon until the liquid is evaporated. Then add 3 tablespoons lard or oil.

2. Fry meat, stirring all the time. Transfer to casserole.

3. In oil, lightly brown consecutively and transfer to casserole: finely chopped onion, diced carrot, diced celery, chopped red peppers (blanched and peeled off), and tomatoes (skinned and coarsely grated.).

4. Season with red and black pepper, chopped parsley and salt to taste.

5. Cover with warm water, add 3 tablespoons lard (or oil), cover with lid and seal up with dough.

6. Bake in a moderate oven. Take the casserole out of oven every 15 minutes, shake and turn it. Check whether dough seal is intact and add a little more dough where necessary to prevent steam go out.

If using cooking foil, take a piece big enough to wrap the whole casserole.

KEBAB ON RICE

INGREDIENTS: 600 g boned pork, 1 1/2 coffee cups lard (butter, oil),
2 onions, 1 tablespoon tomato paste,
1 tablespoon flour, 1/2 teaspoon ground black pepper,
2 coffee cups rice, salt

1. Cut meat in 2 cm cubes, put it in a saucepan and lightly brown in 1 coffee cup oil.

2. Remove meat and lightly brown chopped onions in the same oil.

3. Add tomato paste diluted with 2 coffee cups water, and flour (lightly browned in a dry non-greased frying pan and diluted with 1 coffee cup lukewarm water) and boil, stirring occasionally with an wooden spoon.

4. Put meat, add salt to taste, sprinkle with black pepper and pour in hot water to cover meat.

5. Cover and simmer until meat is done.

6. Fry separately the cleaned, washed and dried rice in the remaining oil for about 10 minutes.

7. Add boiling water (two and a half times more in volume than rice; in this case, 5 coffee cups water for 2 coffee cups rice).

8. Add salt and stew rice in moderate oven for about 20 minutes.

9. Serve meat pieces on rice with sauce from the kebab.

KEBAB IN OMELET

INGREDIENTS:

600 g pork fillet, 2 coffee cups oil, 1 onion,
2 peppers, 2 tomatoes, 1/3 teaspoon ground black pepper,
2 or 3 garlic cloves, 2 tablespoons chopped parsley,
6 eggs, 4 olives,
2 tablespoons flour, salt

1. Cut meat in slices and fry in 1 coffee cup oil. Remove meat from saucepan.

2. Lightly brown in the same oil the finely cut peppers, onion and tomatoes, peeled and coarsely grated.

3. Add finely cut garlic cloves and salt.

4. Return meat, sprinkle with black pepper and chopped parsley.

5. Beat eggs with flour and fry in another frying pan 4 omelets.

6. Put meet and vegetable stuffing on one half of each omelet and fold in two.

7. Put one ring row onion and one pitted olive on each omelet.

MONASTERY GYUVECH WITH PORK

INGREDIENTS:

600 g boned pork, 4–5 onions,

1/2 kg potatoes, 1/2 kg zucchini, 1/4 kg carrots, 1 bulb garlic,

10–12 black peppercorns, 2 bay leaves, salt,

1 bunch parsley, 1 coffee cup oil (or lard)

1. Cut meat in pieces and semi-fry in oil. Transfer to a ceramic casserole or a baking pan.

2. Lightly brown in the same oil onions, cut in thin slices, and add to meat.

3. Lightly brown alternately and add in the ceramic casserole potatoes, zucchini and carrots.

4. Add peeled garlic, crushed with salt, black peppercorns, bay leaves and chopped parsley.

5. Mix well all ingredients and if the casserole does not have a lid, seal it with cooking foil (same applies to the baking pan).

6. Bake in a slow oven for a while, then increase heat. The dish is ready when absorbs all liquids.

GRILLED PORK FILLET

INGREDIENTS FOR 6 SERVINGS:

1 1/4 kg pork fillet,

3 tablespoons oil, 1 tablespoon lemon juice (or vinegar),

3–4 cloves garlic, 1 stalk basil,

1 teaspoon ground black pepper, salt,

2 handfuls mushrooms (fresh or canned), 3 tablespoons butter, 2 onions

1. Cut fillet in pieces, 200 g each and 1 1/2 cm thick. Marinate overnight in oil, lemon juice (vinegar), crushed garlic cloves and basil.

2. Drain meat and sprinkle with salt and black pepper.

3. Cut mushrooms in slices and semi fry in a saucepan with butter and chopped onions until soft.

4. Put some of the mixture on each piece of the fillet, fold it and pin on each side with metal skewers.

5. Brush fillet slices with marinade and grill on both sides.

BAKED PORK RIBS

INGREDIENTS FOR 2 SERVINGS:
4 ribs, 2 tablespoons vinegar, oil, salt

1. Remove membranes and excessive fat from ribs, boil to soften in 1 liter water with vinegar.
2. Heat oil (1/2 cm thick layer) in a baking pan and put in it the drained tenderized ribs.
3. Bake in a hot oven for 15 minutes, then lower heat. Turn the ribs every 10 minutes.
4. The ribs are ready when meat is fully tender. Season with salt and serve hot.

BAKED PORK STEAKS WITH ONION

INGREDIENTS:
4 medium steaks, 1 teaspoon ground black pepper,
1 coffee cup oil,
3 onions (or 1 bunch green onions),
1 cup beer, salt

1. Tenderize steaks by pounding, salt and sprinkle with black pepper.
2. Lightly brown on both sides in hot oil. Put in a baking pan.
3. Lightly brown chopped onions in the same oil and transfer to pan with steaks.
4. Pour in beer (it should cover the steaks) and bake in oven at moderate heat for about 1 hour.
Serve with boiled potatoes, sprinkled with melted butter.

PORK STEAKS WITH FRIED EGGS

INGREDIENTS:
4 steaks, 1 tablespoon lemon juice or vinegar,
1 coffee cup flour, 1 teaspoon ground black pepper,
1 1/2 coffee cups oil (lard, butter), 4 eggs,
4 black peppercorns, salt

1. Tenderize steaks by pounding, sprinkle with lemon juice (or vinegar) and black pepper, roll in flour and fry in 1 coffee cup heated oil.

2. Serve steaks and pour on the oil used for frying.

3. Fry eggs in remaining oil and put one on each steak with one peppercorn in the middle of the yolk of each egg.

MIXED MEAT IN GYUVECHE

INGREDIENTS FOR 12 SERVINGS:
1/2 kg veal, 1/2 kg pork, 3/4 kg mutton, boned meat of 1 chicken,
3 coffee cups oil, 2–3 onions, 3 carrots,
1/2 celery root, 1 tablespoon tomato paste,
1 teaspoon red pepper, 1 teaspoon ground black pepper,
1 cup canned peas, 1 cup canned green beans, 1 green pepper,
6–7 potatoes, 2 tablespoons flour, 3 tablespoons melted butter,
1 liter milk, 5 eggs, 2 bunches parsley, salt

1. Cut meat in bite-size pieces and semi-fry in a saucepan with 2 coffee cups oil (first put pork, then veal, chicken and finally mutton). Remove from saucepan with a slotted spoon and distribute in 12 gyuveche (little ceramic bowls).

2. In the same oil and little water stew for a while chopped onions, sliced carrots and diced celery.

3. Add tomato paste diluted with 1 1/2 coffee cups warm water, red pepper, ground black pepper, canned peas, canned green beans (if peas and green beans are fresh, first cook), green pepper cut in rings, salt to taste.

4. Semi-fry separately in 1 coffee cup oil potatoes, cut in chunks and distribute in the individual bowls.

5. Distribute evenly stewed vegetable mix.

6. Cover the individual bowls with lids and bake in a moderate oven for 1/2 hour.

7. Prepare the following mixture: lightly brown flour in a dry non-greased frying pan and dilute it with 1/2 coffee cup lukewarm water. Lightly brown flour in butter, add milk and beaten eggs.

8. Distribute mixture in the individual bowls and bake for 15 minutes, uncovered.

9. Serve sprinkled with chopped parsley.

Meals with minced meat and internal parts

MINCED MEAT PREPARATION

Minced meat is usually prepared of beef or veal (rarely of lamb or pork). Pork is added to beef or veal if minced meat is to be used for certain dishes, mostly for sarmi (stuffed vine or cabbage leaves), and also for grilled meat balls (kyufteta and kebapcheta). In these cases, pork should not be more than half of the total amount of meat. Good cooks recommend 2/3 veal (or beef) to 1/3 pork as the best proportion.

When preparing minced meat at home, either with hand-operated or electric meat mincer, first remove membranes, sinews and bones of meat. Cut it in 2–3 cm pieces for easier mincing. If minced twice, meat processing is easier and the dishes are far more delicious.

Minced meat mixed with onion should be thermally processed within 3 hours after onion is added. For minced meat preparation use stale bread that has soaked in water or, even better, in milk for 1/2 hour. Drain bread in a strainer (but not completely, to prevent it from turning into a bread ball). When a bigger quantity of minced meat is to be prepared and more than 5 or 6 eggs are needed, use just the white of the additional ones; the yolks may come into use in another dish.

CHIRPANSKI KYUFTETA
(MEAT BALLS WITH TOMATO SAUCE)

INGREDIENTS:
1/2 kg minced meat (mixed), 3 onions, 1 egg, 1 slice white bread,
1/2 bunch parsley, 1/2 teaspoon ground black pepper,
1 coffee cup flour, 1 coffee cup oil,
1 carrot, 1 piece of celery root, 1 teaspoon tomato paste,
1 teaspoon red pepper, 3 peppers (fresh or pickled),
3 potatoes, 2–3 tomatoes (fresh or canned), salt

1. Combine minced meat, 1 chopped onion, bread (soaked in milk or water and drained in a strainer), beaten egg, chopped parsley, black pepper and salt to taste. Mix well.

2. Scoop with wet palms about 70–80 g of the mixture, roll with palms and flatten gently to make oval kyufteta. Roll in flour and semi-fry in oil at high heat. Remove when done.

3. Lightly brown in the same oil 2 chopped onions, carrots and celery, cut into big dices.

4. Add 1 tablespoon flour (lightly browned in a dry non-greased frying pan and diluted with 1 coffee cup lukewarm water) and tomato paste (diluted with 1 coffee cup warm water). Sprinkle with red pepper and add immediately 2 coffee cups hot water.

5. Increase heat. When the sauce comes to boil, add peppers (seeds removed) cut in rings, diced potatoes and the semi-fried meat balls.

6. Salt to taste and simmer under lid for about 20 minutes.

7. The dish can be transferred to a baking pan, covered with thin tomato slices and baked in oven for just 15 minutes.

CABBAGE SARMI
(STUFFED FRESH CABBAGE LEAVES)

INGREDIENTS:
1/2 kg minced meat (mixed), 1 medium cabbage,
1/2 coffee cup vinegar, 1 coffee cup oil, 1 1/2 coffee cups rice,
1 large onion, 1/2 teaspoon ground black pepper, salt

1. Boil cabbage for about 20 minutes in 1 liter water with vinegar.

2. Fry lightly rice and chopped onion in oil. When onion is lightly brown, add minced meat, black pepper, salt to taste and 1 coffee cup warm water. Stir with an wooden spoon and remove from heat when water is absorbed. Leave to cool.

3. Put some of the mixture in the middle of each cabbage leaf and wrap carefully. Cut stems inside each leaf so that it rolls better round the stuffing. Put an inverted plate in a saucepan with large bottom and arrange sarmi on it.

4. Pour in 2 cups of water and simmer under lid until the liquid is absorbed.

For the preparation of sarmi also vine, dock, mountain spinach, beetroot or young lime tree leaves may be used. Wash brined vine leaves with warm water.

Fresh vine leaves must be scalded with boiling water. When folding sarmi, the smooth side of the leaves should remain on the outside. Put filling at the lower part of leaf (from the side of stem) and fold tightly from all sides. The filling may be semi-fried, but it may be used raw too. In the latter case use more oil and water to prevent filling from drying.

Use oil to lightly brown onion if the minced meat is fat, and butter for minced lamb, mutton and lean veal. The spices usually used, are ground black pepper, savoury, chopped fresh parsley and dill.

Serve vine leaves sarmi with yogurt combined with crushed garlic and chopped dill.

LYASKOVSKI SARMI WITH VINE LEAVES

INGREDIENTS:

20 vine leaves,
1/2 kg minced meat (veal-pork mix, but also minced mutton can be used),
2 small (or 1 large) onions, 5 tablespoons oil, 1 coffee cup rice,
1/2 teaspoon ground black pepper, 2 tablespoons chopped parsley,
1 teaspoon tomato paste, salt

1. Put vine leaves in a deep pot and pour in lightly salted boiling water. Leave for 15 minutes, drain and dry with clean towel.

2. For the stuffing: lightly brown chopped onions in 4 tablespoons oil. Add minced meat, fry for a while, add rice and fry lightly. Sprinkle with black pepper and chopped parsley. Simmer covered for about 10 minutes at moderate heat.

3. Put one scalded vine leave on your palm with the face down, put some stuffing on it and tightly fold it.

4. Put the excess vine leaves on the bottom of a large saucepan, place sarmi in saucepan and cover with an inverted porcelain plate. If there are no vine leaves left, grease the bottom of saucepan with oil or put on it an inverted plate.

5. Add tomato paste mixed with 1 tablespoon oil and boiled for a few minutes.

6. Pour in warm water and simmer covered with lid for about 1 hour.
Serve warm.

MOUSSAKA WITH POTATOES

INGREDIENTS:
1/2 kg minced meat (mixed), 600 g potatoes,
1 coffee cup oil, 3 onions, 2 teaspoons tomato paste,
6 tomatoes (fresh or canned), 1 tablespoon chopped parsley,
1 teaspoon red pepper, 1/2 teaspoon ground black pepper,
2 coffee cups milk, 1 tablespoon flour, 1 egg,
2 tablespoons finely grated kashkaval (yellow cheese), salt

1. Lightly brown chopped onions in oil in a saucepan. Add tomato paste diluted with 1 1/2 coffee cups lukewarm water, minced meat, 3 tomatoes (peeled and coarsely grated) and chopped parsley.

2. Cover with lid and simmer for about 10 minutes, remove lid and keep on heat until all the liquid is evaporated.

3. Add red and black pepper, salt, mix well and add diced potatoes.

4. In a greased baking pan layer remaining tomatoes (peeled and sliced). Pour mixture on them.

5. Bake in a moderate oven until the surface is golden.

6. Pour over the following mixture: lightly brown flour in a dry non-greased frying pan and add it to milk, put in beaten egg and grated kashkaval. Bake for another 15 minutes.

GARDENER'S MOUSSAKA

INGREDIENTS:
4–5 potatoes, 1/2 kg minced meat (mixed), 2 onions,
2 coffee cups oil, 1/2 teaspoon ground black pepper,
1 teaspoon red pepper, 2 aubergines, 2 medium zucchini,
2 tomatoes, 1 tablespoon chopped mint, 2 eggs,
1 tablespoon flour, 1 cup yogurt,
1 tablespoon chopped parsley, salt

1. Peel potatoes and cut in slices, fry only on one side in 1 coffee cup very hot oil.

2. Arrange in a layer in a greased baking pan with the fried side to bottom.

3. Fry separately minced meat with chopped onions in 1/2 coffee cup oil.

Salt to taste and add black and red pepper. Fry until the liquid is evaporated. Remove from heat and add chopped parsley.

4. Peel aubergines zebra like: in 2–3 cm wide strips. Salt peeled parts and leave in a tilted baking pan for 1 hour until bitter juice is drained. Dice and fry in the oil used for frying of potatoes.

5. Put in a baking pan a thin layer of fried minced meat atop potatoes. Put one layer of fried aubergines and one layer of minced meat. Then add a layer of zucchini – peeled, diced and lightly fried in 1/2 coffee cup oil. Put another layer of minced meat. Cover with tomatoes, sliced and sprinkled with chopped mint. Pour in the oil used for frying of the vegetables, some hot water and bake in a preheated oven.

6. When ready, pour over mixture, prepared of beaten eggs, flour (lightly browned in a dry non-greased frying pan) and yogurt. Bake for a few more minutes.

When preparing moussaka, a layer of peppers (baked, peeled and cut in small pieces) may be added.

STUFFED GREEN PEPPERS

INGREDIENTS:
10–12 large long peppers, 1/2 kg minced meat (mixed),
2 onions, 6 tablespoons oil, 3 tablespoons rice,
2 tomatoes, 1/2 teaspoon ground black pepper,
1 teaspoon red pepper, salt

In the autumn most suitable for stuffing are red or bell peppers, and in the summer – green peppers.

1. Cut lids of peppers with the stem, remove seeds.

2. Lightly brown chopped onions in 5 tablespoons oil. Add rice and 1 coffee cup warm water. Fry for 4–5 minutes, stirring with an wooden spoon, then add peeled and coarsely grated tomatoes, fry at moderate heat for about 10 more minutes. Add minced meat, salt to taste and black pepper. Keep on heat, stirring until minced meat becomes white (do not fry it though). If mixture is too thick, add some warm water.

3. Remove from heat, leave to cool and stuff peppers, leaving some space for the rice to swell.

4. Put peppers with the opening up in a shallow saucepan; in this case it is not necessary to put a plate atop of them. Pour in water to cover peppers to the middle,

cover with lid and simmer, adding occasionally some warm water.

5. Peppers are ready when rice is soft. Fry red pepper in 1 tablespoon oil and add in a thin stream. Do not stir, just sway saucepan.

Serve stuffed peppers with yogurt.

KEBAPCHETA AND KYUFTETA
(GRILLED MEAT BALLS)

Kebapcheta and kyufteta are a meat dish, typical for Bulgaria and for the Balkans. They are made of different types of meat. The difference between kebapcheta and kyufteta is mostly in their shape – kyufteta are flat meat balls with the size of a small apple. Kebapcheta are made of the same quantity minced meat but they are 10–15 cm long, with cylindrical shape.

Minced meat for kebapcheta and kyufteta is prepared in the same way. It is named after the meat prevailing in its preparation – lamb, mutton, goat, veal, beef or pork minced meat. Usually the lean meat is mixed with pork or veal. A good combination is, for example, 2/3 lamb and 1/3 beef (or veal, mutton, goat). The most frequently used minced meat is 2/3 beef (veal) and 1/3 pork.

To prepare minced meat for meat balls, mix very well 1 kg minced meat with 1 teaspoon salt, 1 teaspoon ground black pepper, 1/2 teaspoon ground cumin, and 1/2 teaspoon crushed savoury. Leave it in a cool place for a few hours.

While mixing the minced meat, except for the above mentioned spices, also 1 medium chopped onion may be added to 750 g minced meat. The same quantity minced meat absorbs 1 coffee cup water, while mixing it.

To shape kyufteta for grilling, dip your palms in a solution of equal portions of water and vinegar, scoop one handful minced meat, roll a ball and flatten to round or oval shape.

Kebapcheta are prepared in the same way but they are rolled in a cylindrical shape on a bread–board, wetted with solution of water and vinegar.

Hot kyufteta are prepared by adding chopped chili pepper to the minced meat, along with the other spices.

Serve kebapcheta and kyufteta with vegetable salad and French fries or boiled potatoes.

DRYANOVSKI GRILLED KYUFTETA

INGREDIENTS:
1/2 kg minced meat (mixed), 1 small onion,
1 teaspoon cumin (baked and ground),
1/2 teaspoon ground black pepper, 1 slice white bread (crust removed),
1 coffee cup milk or water, salt

1. Soak bread in water, drain it in a strainer but leave it wet, add it to minced meat along with chopped onion, cumin, black pepper, milk (or water) and salt to taste.
2. Mix minced meat with palms wetted in a solution of equal portions of water and vinegar. Shape oval kyufteta and flatten.
3. Heat grill and grease rods with tallow or fresh bacon. Grill kyufteta on both sides.
4. Serve hot with season garnish – baked peppers, tomatoes, lyutenitsa (See Lyutenitsa), white beans, French fries.

GRILLED KYUFTETA WITH KASHKAVAL

Prepare kyufteta following the above recipe. Put inside each one 1 teaspoon diced kashkaval (yellow cheese).

YAMBOLSKI GRILLED KEBAPCHETA

INGREDIENTS FOR 8 SERVINGS:
700 g boned veal, 300 g boned pork,
1 teaspoon salt, 1/2 teaspoon ground cumin,
1–2 coffee cups beer, 1 small onion, 1 teaspoon ground black pepper

1. Mince meat and mix in salt, black pepper and cumin.
2. Keep mixing with one hand and with the other pour in as much beer as the mixture takes in. Baked and crushed chili peppers may be added too.
3. Leave minced meat in a cool place for 24 hours.

4. On the next day add chopped onion (optional).

5. Mix minced meat with water (as much as it takes in).

6. Roll kebapcheta and grill on hot grill with rods greased with tallow or a piece of fresh bacon.

GRILLED INN-KEEPER'S KYUFTETA

INGREDIENTS FOR 5 KYUFTETA:

1/2 kg minced meat (mixed), 1 small onion,

1/2 teaspoon ground black pepper,

1/2 teaspoon grounded or crushed cumin,

2 handfuls mushrooms (fresh or canned), 2 teaspoons butter,

50 g kashkaval (yellow cheese), salt

1. Mix minced meat, chopped onion, black pepper, cumin and salt to taste.

2. Make 5 small flat loaves with a pit in the middle. Fill the pit with 1 teaspoon mushrooms (finely cut and stewed in butter) and a few dices kashkaval. Cover pit with minced meat.

3. Flatten carefully and grill on a very hot grill.

FRIED KYUFTETA

INGREDIENTS:

1/2 kg minced meat, 1 small onion,

1/2 teaspoon ground black pepper, 1/2 teaspoon ground or crushed cumin,

1 teaspoon crushed savoury, 2 tablespoons chopped parsley,

1 pinch grated nutmeg, 1 egg, 1 slice white bread (crust removed),

1 coffee cup flour, 2 coffee cups oil, salt

1. Mix minced meat with chopped onion, black pepper, cumin, savoury, chopped parsley, nutmeg and salt to taste.

2. Add beaten egg and white bread (soaked in milk or water and drained in a strainer).

3. Mix well, shape in kyufteta, roll in flour and fry in heated oil on both sides turning them carefully with a metal blade or fork, without piercing.

LAMB DROB-SARMA

INGREDIENTS:
about 800 g lamb internal parts – lungs, liver, small intestines, etc.,
2 bunches green onions, 1 coffee cup oil,
1 coffee cup rice, 1/2 teaspoon ground black pepper,
1 lamb mesentery, 1 tomato, 2 tablespoons melted butter,
1 egg, 1 cup yogurt, 1 tablespoon flour, salt

1. Turn the small intestines inside out with a thin stick, wash thoroughly and boil with other parts in lightly salted water until tender. Remove from saucepan and cut in small pieces. Reserve stock.
2. Cut finely green onions and stew in oil to soften.
3. Add rice, chopped parts, black pepper and salt to taste. Fry for a while.
4. Pour in filtered stock to cover the stuffing so prepared. Boil for 15 minutes at moderate heat.
5. Cut lamb mesentery in 4–5 squares and wash thoroughly. Put a slice of tomato and some stuffing in each piece of mesentery and fold to make a round sarma. Instead of tomato, 1 tablespoon tomato paste diluted with some warm water may be added to stuffing while stewing.
6. Arrange in a baking pan greased with melted butter, pour in filtered stock to half-cover them, and bake in a moderate oven.
7. When ready, pour on drob-sarma beaten egg mixed with yogurt (and flour lightly browned in a dry non-greased frying pan, optional). Return to oven for 10 more minutes.
If lamb mesentery is not available, use large serving spoon (or a small ladle) to scoop some stuffing and arrange the scoops tightly in a greased baking pan. Pour over mixture made of 1 tablespoon flour, 2 tablespoons butter and 1 cup milk.

FRIED VEAL LIVER WITH SMOKED BACON

INGREDIENTS:
800 g veal liver, 1 coffee cup flour, 100 g smoked bacon,
1 coffee cup red wine, 2 tablespoons chopped parsley, 2 coffee cups oil

1. Fry in oil liver, cut into pieces.
2. Slice smoked bacon in thin strips and put in a heated non-greased frying

pan. Remove with a slotted spoon when lightly browned, pour in the frying pan wine and the oil from the fried liver, cover and boil for 5–6 minutes.

3. Remove lid and boil for another 5–6 minutes. Serve liver in warm plates sprinkled with fried strips smoked bacon and wine sauce. Sprinkle with chopped parsley.

BAKED VEAL TRIPE

INGREDIENTS:
800 g veal tripe, 1 teaspoon tomato paste,
1 coffee cup melted butter, 10–12 black peppercorns,
1 teaspoon red pepper, 1/2 teaspoon ground black pepper, salt

1. Boil tripe for 3–4 hours (1 1/2 hours in a pressure cooker). Cut in strips with scissors or knife.

2. Pour on tripe enough water to cover it, salt to taste and cook at moderate heat.

3. When water comes to boil, add tomato paste diluted with 1 coffee cup warm water, and boil for only 5 minutes.

4. Pour in a baking pan, add melted butter and black peppercorns. Bake in oven for 15 minutes.

5. Serve warm sprinkled with red and black pepper.

BOILED VEAL TONGUE WITH SAUCE

INGREDIENTS:
800 g veal tongue, 2 onions, 3 carrots,
1 parsley root, 1 piece of celery (or parsnip),
3 tablespoons oil, 1 teaspoon tomato paste,
2 coffee cups white wine, salt

1. Scrape tongue well and wash thoroughly, drain, rub with salt and put in a saucepan. Cover with hot water. Add 1 onion cut into two, 2 whole carrots, parsley root and piece of celery (parsnip). Boil at moderate heat. Reserve stock.

2. Peel off boiled tongue, cut it into slices and arrange in an oval plate.

3. Prepare the following sauce: fry lightly in oil 1 chopped onion, add 1 diced carrot and lastly – flour (lightly browned in a dry non-greased frying pan and diluted with 1 coffee cup lukewarm water). Add tomato paste diluted with 1 coffee cup warm water. Pour in wine and simmer uncovered until the sauce comes to boil. Add 1/2 cup stock, cover and boil for another 10 minutes.

4. Filter sauce, salt to taste and pour it over boiled tongue.

The dish may be served garnished with pickled cucumbers and potato puree.

PACHA
(COLD PORK JELLY)

INGREDIENTS FOR 8 SERVINGS:
1 kg pig head and pig knuckles, 3 carrots, 1 piece of celery,
10–12 seed onions, 2 hard-boiled eggs,
parsley leaves, celery leaves,
salt, vinegar, garlic

1. Put head and knuckles in a saucepan, pour in cold water. Cook until water comes to boil, pour out water, pour in again fresh cold water and boil until ready. Drain, bone and cut meat in small bite-size pieces.

2. Filter stock, bring it to boil and add the cut meat, diced carrots and celery, seed onions.

3. Dice eggs.

4. Brush with cold water bottom and sides of the dishes, prepared for jelly, and distribute cut eggs in them.

5. Remove meat and vegetables from stock with the help of a slotted spoon and distribute in the dishes.

6. Put parsley leaves and chopped celery leaves in stock and distribute in the dishes. Add vinegar to taste to each dish. Crushed garlic diluted with vinegar may be added.

7. When the stock cools down and turns into jelly, it may be transferred to plates. For this purpose, first dip dishes in warm water and turn on plates.

Fish, mussels and snails

FISH STEW
(WITH FRESHWATER, SEA OR OCEAN FISH)

INGREDIENTS:
1 kg fish, 2–3 onions, 3–4 tablespoons oil,
1 tablespoon flour, 1 teaspoon tomato paste (or 2–3 tomatoes),
1 teaspoon ground black pepper, 1 teaspoon crushed thyme,
1 carrot, 2–3 bay leaves, 1 teaspoon chopped celery leaves,
1 teaspoon chopped parsley, salt

1. Use fish with big fishbone. Clean it, sprinkle with black pepper, salt and leave in a cold place for 2–3 hours.

2. Boil onions, cut in slices, in some lightly salted water, stirring occasionally with an wooden spoon.

3. When the liquid evaporates and onion becomes tender, ad oil and lightly brown.

4. Lightly brown flour in a dry non-greased frying pan, dilute it with 1 coffee cup water and add to onion. Add tomato paste diluted with 1 coffee cup warm water (or peeled and coarsely grated tomatoes). Put in carrot cut in thin slices, bay leaves, dried and crushed thyme, celery leaves and parsley. Pour in warm water, cover and simmer until sauce thickens.

5. Add fish cut in pieces (leave smaller fish whole), salt to taste and simmer covered for about 20 minutes.

FISH PLAKIA WITH WINE

INGREDIENTS:
1 kg fish, 4 onions, 2–3 medium carrots,
1 celery root, 2 coffee cups oil, 2 tomatoes, 6–7 cloves garlic,
10 black peppercorns, 1 bay leave, pinch of thyme,
1 coffee cup white wine, 1/2 lemon,
3 tablespoons chopped parsley, salt, flour

1. Chop onions, dice carrots and celery. Stew in 1 coffee cup oil.

2. Add 1 peeled and coarsely grated tomato (fresh or canned), chopped garlic cloves, black pepper, bay leave and thyme. Salt to taste.

3. Pour in white wine and 1 cup warm water or fish stock. Transfer to a baking pan and arrange atop fish, cut in pieces and rolled in flour.

4. Sway the baking pan and put one lemon slice and 1 tomato slice on each fish piece. Sprinkle with chopped parsley, add 1 coffee cup oil and bake in a moderate oven.

RIBNIK
(FISH BAKED IN DOUGH)

INGREDIENTS FOR 8 SERVINGS:

1 carp about 1 kg;

for the stuffing – 1 coffee cup melted butter, 3 onions, 1 dried red pepper, 2–3 tomatoes (fresh or canned), 1 tablespoon dried savoury, 1 tablespoon dried (or fresh) parsley, 1 cup ground walnuts;

for the dough – 600–700 g flour, 1 tablespoon vinegar, 1 tablespoon oil, pinch of salt and pinch of ground black pepper

1. Clean and wash carp, dry it with a clean towel, salt from inside and outside, leave in a cold place for 3–4 hours.

2. Stuffing preparation: lightly brown chopped onions in hot butter. Add some water and dry red pepper (soaked in hot water, peeled and torn in small pieces). Put in tomatoes, peeled and coarsely grated, and spices. Remove from heat and cool, then add ground walnuts.

3. Sift twice flour in a baking pan. Make a well in the middle of flour and put in it vinegar, oil, salt and black pepper. Pour in water and first mix with spoon, then with floured hands and knead medium hard dough. Leave it to rest in a warm place for 1/2 hour.

4. Stuff carp.

5. Roll out dough in a thick crust and put it in a greased baking pan. Put stuffed carp in the middle and fold ends of dough like an envelope; brush with oil.

6. Pour in water to make 1 cm layer and bake in a moderate oven, basting occasionally dough with sauce from the baking pan.

Serve cooled.

CARP GYUVECH

INGREDIENTS:

1 kg carp, 2 tablespoons oil, 1 onion,

1 carrot, piece of celery root, 1 parsley root,

1 teaspoon tomato paste (or 3 fresh or canned tomatoes),

1 coffee cup canned peas, 1/2 cup canned green beans,

5–6 black peppercorns, salt

1. Clean, wash and dry carp. Cut in pieces, salt and leave aside for 1/2 hour.

2. Lightly brown alternately in oil and transfer to a ceramic casserole (or baking pan): onion cut in thin slices, chopped carrot and chopped celery piece, tomato paste diluted with 1 coffee cup warm water (or the peeled and coarsely grated tomatoes), canned peas and canned green beans (if fresh, boil the peas and green beans separately).

3. Add black peppercorns, put in carp pieces, pour in some water and bake in a moderate oven.

FRIED CARP WITH GARLIC SAUCE

INGREDIENTS:

1 kg carp, 3 tablespoons flour, 1 coffee cup butter,

1/2 bunch parsley, 4–5 cloves garlic,

salt, oil, lemon juice

1. Cut carp in pieces, roll in flour mixed with salt and fry in very hot oil

2. Pour hot butter on fried fish and sprinkle with lemon juice and chopped parsley.

3. Lightly brown crushed garlic in the oil used for frying, and pour on fish.

FRIED GOBY

INGREDIENTS:

1 kg goby (Black Sea fish), 3 coffee cups flour,

3 coffee cups oil, salt

1. Clean, wash and dry fish with a towel. Salt and leave aside for 10 minutes to take in the salt. If not well salted, the fish will fall apart during frying.

2. Roll in flour and fry in hot oil.

3. Fry only 4–5 fish at a time, otherwise oil temperature lowers and it is harder to form crust. Fry fish on both sides, turning each only once. First fry at high heat, then at moderate and even heat. When a ready fish is removed, move in its place a fish that is being fried next to it, and put a new one in its place.

Serve warm, sprinkled with lemon juice.

FRIED TURBOT

INGREDIENTS:
turbot, flour, oil, lemon, parsley, salt

1. Clean fish, peel off skin, cut into pieces, wash and salt. Leave aside for about 10 minutes to take in salt.

2. Roll in flour and fry in very hot oil

3. Sprinkle with chopped parsley and with lemon juice. Decorate with lemon slices.

GRILLED SMALL BLACK SEA BLUE FISH, MACKEREL OR SCAD

INGREDIENTS:
1 kg fish, 1 1/2 teaspoons ground black pepper,
1 1/2 coffee cups oil, salt

1. Clean fish and cut into pieces, dry in a towel, salt and sprinkle with black pepper. Leave aside for 1/2 hour.

2. Cover grill with greased cooking foil, dip fish in oil and arrange on the grill. Serve fish with appropriate sauce.

GRILLED TROUT

Ingredients:

4 trout fishes, 1 1/2 teaspoons ground black pepper,
1 coffee cup melted butter, 2 handfuls mushrooms (fresh or canned),
1 teaspoon dried thyme, 1/2 lemon, salt

1. Clean, wash and dry fish, salt and sprinkle with black pepper from inside and outside.
2. Cut mushrooms in small pieces and stew in butter, then salt to taste and sprinkle with black pepper and thyme. Leave to cool.
3. Stuff fish with the mixture thus prepared.
4. Cover the heated grill with greased cooking foil and arrange fish on it. Peel lemon, cut it in slices, and put a slice on each fish. Grill for about 20 minutes.

FISH PANCAKES

Ingredients:

1/2 kg fish fillet, 1 onion, 1 carrot;
for the pancake batter – 4 eggs, 1 cup flour,
2 cups milk, 1/2 teaspoon ground black pepper;
1 coffee cup oil, salt

1. Bake onion and carrot on a hot plate or in oven, then boil with fish fillet at moderate heat in lightly salted water for about 20 minutes.
2. Drain fillet and cut it in small pieces.
3. Prepare thin pancake batter with beaten eggs, flour and milk. Add fish, black pepper and salt to taste.
4. Heat oil and bake pancakes, scooping with a ladle from mixture.
Serve with pickled cucumbers and a lemon slice.

SNAILS WITH SPICY SAUCE

INGREDIENTS:
the meat of 30 boiled snails,
4 tablespoons oil, 2 teaspoons mustard, 2 teaspoons vinegar,
1/2 teaspoon ground black pepper, 2 tablespoons flour,
2 tablespoons chopped parsley, salt

1. Put in heated oil mustard, vinegar and flour (lightly browned in a dry non-greased frying pan and diluted with 1 coffee cup lukewarm water).

2. Fry until flour is lightly brown, then remove from heat, salt to taste, add black pepper and beat to mix well. Add chopped parsley.

3. Pour this sauce on snail meat cut in small pieces.

MUSSELS FRIED IN FLOUR AND EGGS

INGREDIENTS FOR 2 SERVINGS:
meat of 250 mussels;

for the marinade – 1 coffee cup white wine,
1 tablespoon lemon juice (or a pinch of salt of lemon diluted with little water),
2 tablespoons oil, 1/3 teaspoon salt,
1 tablespoon chopped parsley, 1 bay leaf;

for the pancake batter – 5 tablespoons flour, 1 egg,
milk (as much as the mix would take in); 1 1/2 coffee cups oil,
1/2 lemon, 1 coffee cup bread crumbs

1. Prepare marinade by mixing the products.

2. Boil mussels, then marinade for 30 minutes. If mussels are canned, put them directly in the marinade.

3. Prepare thin pancake batter.

4. Dip mussels one by one in batter, roll in bread crumbs and fry in very hot oil.

5. Put fried mussels on an inverted metal sifter to drain oil.
Serve with lemon slices.

Meals with poultry

CHICKEN STEW WITH WINE

INGREDIENTS:
1 chicken, 2 coffee cups flour, 1 1/2 coffee cups oil,
2 onions, 1 garlic bulb,
10 black peppercorns, 1 tablespoon crushed dried savoury,
1 coffee cup white wine, 1/2 bunch parsley, salt

1. Cut chicken in portions, roll in flour and fry on each side in very hot oil until golden. Remove from pan.
2. Fry chopped onions in the same oil.
3. Add fried chicken, finely cut garlic, black pepper, salt to taste and savoury. Pout in wine and add water to cover 2/3 of the products.
4. Cover and stew at moderate heat until meat is fully tender.
5. When ready, add chopped parsley.

AUBERGINES STUFFED WITH CHICKEN MEAT

INGREDIENTS:
1 chicken, 4 medium aubergines,
3 tablespoons butter, 1 onion, 2–3 tomatoes,
1 teaspoon ground black pepper,
2 handfuls mushrooms (fresh or canned),
juice from 1 lemon (or a pinch of salt of lemon diluted with some water),
salt;
for the final mixture – 4 eggs, 1 cup yogurt

1. Peel off aubergines, sprinkle with some salt and leave for 1 hour in a tilted backing pan for the bitter juice to drain. Then cut each aubergine lengthwise in two and remove pulp.
2. Boil chicken in lightly salted water, bone and mince meat.
3. Mince aubergine pulp.

4. Lightly brown alternately in butter chopped onion, minced chicken meat, minced aubergine pulp and peeled and coarsely grated tomatoes, stirring with an wooden spoon. Salt and add black pepper.

5. Add mushrooms (scalded and cut in small pieces). Keep stirring, add lemon juice (or salt of lemon diluted with some water).

6. Stuff aubergines with this mixture and arrange in a greased backing pan. Pour extra stuffing around aubergines. Add warm water to cover 2/3 of the products and bake for about 20 minutes in a moderate oven.

7. Pour over the final mixture, prepared of beaten eggs and yogurt, and bake for another 5–6 minutes.

FRIED CHICKEN

INGREDIENTS:
1 chicken, 2 coffee cups flour, 1 egg,
2 coffee cups bread crumbs, 2 coffee cups melted butter (or oil), salt

1. Remove breast bone, cut chicken in 4 portions and rub with salt.
2. Roll in flour, dip in beaten egg, roll in bread crumbs and fry in very hot oil on all sides until golden.
3. Serve with boiled potatoes, sprinkled with chopped parsley.

GRILLED CHICKEN WITH SAUCE

INGREDIENTS:
1 chicken, 2 tablespoons melted butter, salt;

for the sauce – 100 g mayonnaise, 1 tablespoon mustard,
1 tablespoon drained yogurt (See Snezhanka salad),
1 small onion, 1 tablespoon chopped parsley,
2 hard–boiled eggs, 1 tablespoon lemon juice (or apple vinegar), salt

1. Half–boil chicken in lightly salted water. Drain and dry chicken.
2. Rub with melted butter and grill on all sides on very hot grill until golden.
3. Prepare sauce by mixing mayonnaise with mustard, yogurt, grated onion, chopped parsley, diced boiled eggs, lemon juice (or apple vinegar) and salt to taste.

CHICKEN LIVER IN GYUVECHE

INGREDIENTS:

16 livers, 3 tablespoons butter (or oil),

2 handfuls mushrooms (fresh or canned), 1 onion, 4 eggs,

1 teaspoon ground black pepper, salt

1. Grill livers.

2. Cut mushrooms in small pieces and stew in butter (or oil).

3. Cut onion in thin slices, crush gently with some salt and distribute in 4 gyuveche (little ceramic bowls).

4. Distribute mushrooms and livers. Put all bowls in cold oven, increase heat and bake for about 20 minutes at high heat.

5. Add one egg in each bowl (do not stir), salt to taste and sprinkle black pepper. Bake for just a few more minutes or until the white of the eggs is barely cooked.

STEWED TURKEY WITH PLUMS

INGREDIENTS:

1 kg turkey meat, 1 1/2 coffee cups oil,

3 onions, 1 teaspoon tomato paste, 1 teaspoon red pepper,

1 tablespoon flour, 2 handfuls dried plums, salt

1. Cut meat in portions, fry in oil until golden.

2. Add and lightly brown chopped onion.

3. Add tomato paste diluted with 1 coffee cup warm water. Boil until it turns in grains and add warm water to cover meat.

4. Simmer, covered, until meat softens.

5. Add red pepper and flour (lightly browned in a dry non-greased frying pan and diluted with 1 coffee cup lukewarm water). Salt and stew at low heat.

6. When meat is done, add plums (soaked for 1 hour in warm water and pitted). Cook for another 10 minutes.

Serve warm.

SARMI WITH CHOPPED TURKEY MEAT

INGREDIENTS:
1/2 kg boiled turkey meat, 1 teaspoon red pepper,
1 teaspoon ground black pepper, 6–8 dried red peppers,
large leaves of 1 sour cabbage, 2 tablespoons butter, salt

1. Chop boiled meat with chopper or large knife and stew for a while with butter. Sprinkle red pepper and half of black pepper. Salt to taste and stir well.

2. Put dried red peppers in cold water for 2–3 hours.

3. Instead of sour cabbage, fresh one may be used. In this case, boil the large leaves for about 10 minutes in water with vinegar. Cut off the thick part of leaves, put some meat in the middle of each leaf and fold tightly into sarmi. Stuff red peppers with meat too.

4. Put an inverted plate in a saucepan. Arrange sarmi on it and put stuffed peppers among them. Put an inverted plate on top to press sarmi.

5. Pour in equal parts of water and sour cabbage juice or just water to reach 3–4 cm below the upper plate.

6. Boil at low heat until sarmi are soft.

7. Serve warm, sprinkled with remaining ground black pepper and with sauce from cooking.

ROAST TURKEY
STUFFED WITH SOUR CABBAGE

INGREDIENTS FOR 18 SERVINGS:
1 turkey (or turkey–cock) about 4 kg with the giblets, 5–6 onions,
1 1/2 coffee cups butter, 2 coffee cups rice,
1 handful raisins, 1 teaspoon ground black pepper,
100 g salted bacon, 1 sour cabbage, 1 coffee cup oil

1. Remove thick membrane of gizzard and boil it with the heart; cut all giblets in small pieces (including liver).

2. Prepare stuffing by stewing in butter chopped onions and giblets cut in small pieces.

3. Add washed and dried rice. In Southern Bulgaria raisins are added to the stuffing too.

4. Pour in 1 cup warm water and sprinkle with black pepper. Simmer under lid for about 10 minutes.

5. Stuff turkey while stuffing is still warm. Do not fill the whole cavity – there must be some space left, otherwise stuffing will turn into a ball. Stitch up opening with white thread and tie up the legs to the body with a double thread.

6. Put vine branches (or salted bacon slices) on bottom of a large baking pan and put turkey on them. Pour in water to make 3 cm layer. Cover turkey with long slices of salted bacon and stick them with thick toothpicks. Wrap turkey with large sour cabbage leaves.

7. Roast in very hot oven. Turn turkey every 15 minutes and baste with sauce from the baking pan.

8. Cut remaining sour cabbage in strips and stew in oil.

9. When turkey turns lightly brown, arrange cabbage around it and bake until both turkey and cabbage are done and brown.

10. Serve in baking pan, remove threads and cut in portions.

Turkey can be served with pickles and sour cabbage, sprinkled with red pepper, in addition to baked cabbage.

ROAST DUCK

INGREDIENTS FOR 18 SERVINGS:
1 duck about 4 kg, 2 teaspoons ground black pepper,
1 cup white wine, 1 tablespoon flour, pinch of thyme,
pinch of oregano, salt

1. Wash duck thoroughly and pat dry. Rub from inside and outside with salt and half of the ground black pepper. Tie legs to the body with double white thread and put it in a baking pan with breasts to bottom.

2. Roast at high heat in a preheated oven for about 2 hours. Turn duck every 15 minutes to roast on all sides, and baste with hot water (use altogether 1 cup of water) and with juices from the baking pan.

3. Lower heat and continue to roast at low heat. Keep turning duck every 15 minutes, basting with sauce from baking pan. To check if duck is ready, pierce breasts with a fork; the juice that comes out should be clear. Turn off heat.

4. Filter sauce from the baking pan, put duck in baking pan and return in the warm oven.

5. In a saucepan bring to boil sauce from the baking pan adding white wine. Salt to taste and add remaining black pepper, thyme and oregano. Add flour (lightly browned in a dry non-greased frying pan). Boil for a while and serve duck with the sauce thus prepared.

Garnish with boiled potatoes and season salad.

ROAST PARTRIDGES

1. Pluck feathers, remove giblets and singe partridges. Cut off heads and legs.

2. Dry cavity of each partridge and pat dry livers with a towel. Put one liver in the cavity of each partridge. Stuff in about 100 g diced salted bacon.

3. Wrap each partridge in vine leaves and brush with butter or oil.

4. Now wrap each partridge in wide bacon slices and tie with white thread.

5. Arrange partridges in a generously greased baking pan and roast for 1/2 hour in hot oven, turning them every 10 minutes.

6. Remove bacon and vine leaves. Return partridges in the oven and roast on all sides until they turn red.

7. Cut ready partridges in portions and serve with bacon slices.

STEWED PIGEONS WITH MUSHROOMS

INGREDIENTS:
2 pigeons, 3 tablespoons butter,
250 g mushrooms (fresh or canned),
1 coffee cup oil (or butter),
1 teaspoon ground black pepper, 1/4 kg seed onions,
5–6 black peppercorns, 1/2 teaspoon salt

1. Cut mushrooms in strips and stew in 3 tablespoons butter.

2. Clean, wash and dry pigeons, salt from inside and outside, rub with ground black pepper and fry in another dish in oil (or butter), turning them on all sides.

3. When pigeons are lightly brown, add seed onions and fry for a while.

4. Add mushrooms, black peppercorns and salt.

5. Pour in warm water to cover the products and stew at low heat.

Bread and cakes

NEW YEAR POGACHA (BREAD)

INGREDIENTS:
600–700 g flour, 1 egg, 1 cup milk, 1 cup yogurt,
1 tablespoon vinegar, 1 teaspoon salt, 1 teaspoon baking soda,
1 tablespoon melted lard (or oil)

1. Sift flour twice in a round baking pan.
2. In a separate bowl beat eggs with milk and yogurt (it is possible to use just milk or just yogurt; if neither is available – use 2 cups lukewarm water).
3. Make a well in the sifted flour and pour in it egg mixture. Add vinegar, salt and baking soda. Stir first with a spoon, then knead dough until bubbles start forming in it.
4. Cover dough with a towel and leave it at room temperature for about 1/2 hour.
5. Knead again for a while. Put aside some dough for decoration – make sun, birds, geometric figures.
6. Grease the baking pan with melted lard (or with oil), put in dough, decorate it with figures and bake in a moderate oven.

HOME-MADE PASTRY SHEETS

INGREDIENTS:
1 1/2 kg flour, 2 1/2 cups water,
1 1/2 teaspoons salt, 1 1/2 tablespoons oil

1. Sift flour on a smooth table or on a special board for dough kneading. Make a well in the middle of flour and put salt and oil in it.
2. Knead dough with one hand and with the other pour in water (not very warm). The dough should be neither very hard, nor very soft.
3. Knead with floured hands until dough becomes homogeneous and starts forming bubbles.

4. Cut dough in four balls, put them in a deep greased saucepan (so that dough would not stick). Cover with a damp warm towel. Leave aside for 1/2 hour.

5. Cover table with a clean tablecloth, sprinkle it with a thin layer of flour and roll out on it one of the balls with a rolling pin into a sheet 25 cm in diameter. Then pull sheet on tablecloth in all directions, circling around the table. Leave sheet to dry and cut into pieces with size to choice. Then roll out the other balls.

6. The ready sheets may be put in thin layers and dried. When dry, arrange on a clean sheet of paper and pack. Keep in a dry place – this way they may be preserved for months.

BANITSA (PHYLLO PIE)

PREPARATION:

First method: Take 12 pastry sheets (phyllo). Grease bottom of a pan with butter or oil. Brush 3 sheets with butter. Place sheets one atop the other. Spread 1/3 of filling. Top with 2 more sheets, each brushed with butter or oil. Spread second third of filling. Repeat one more time. Top last layer of filling with 3 oiled sheets. Bake in a moderate oven until a wooden pick inserted in center comes out clean.

Second method: Grease bottom of a pan. Place in pan half of sheets (5 or 6) atop of each other, brushing each with butter or oil. Spread filling. Top with remaining 5–6 sheets, each brushed with butter or oil. Bake in a moderate oven.

BANITSA FILLINGS

Cheese filling

INGREDIENTS:
4 eggs, pinch of baking soda, 1/4 kg sirene (white cheese)

Beat eggs, add baking soda. Keep beating and add crumbed (or grated, or crushed) cheese.

Spinach filling

INGREDIENTS:
1/2 kg spinach, 1/2 cup yogurt, 1 coffee cup oil (or melted butter),
1 teaspoon salt, 1 cup crumbed sirene (white cheese), 3 eggs

1. Squeeze gently water from spinach (washed and cut in strips). Stew in oil (or melted butter). Leave to cool.
2. Stir in cheese, eggs and yogurt.

Filling with minced meat

INGREDIENTS:
1/2 kg minced meat, 100 g butter (or lard),
1 onion, 1 teaspoon ground black pepper

1. Fry lightly chopped onion in butter (or lard), add minced meat and semi-fry. Sprinkle with black pepper.
2. Leave filling to cool before use.

Filling with leaks and rice

INGREDIENTS:
1/2 kg leaks, 1 coffee cup rice, 1/2 cup oil,
1/2 teaspoon ground black pepper, salt

1. Chop leaks and stew in oil.
2. Add rice and fry lightly. Pour in 2 coffee cups warm water and cook until water is absorbed.
3. Sprinkle with black pepper and salt to taste.
Use filling cooled.

TUTMANIK
(CHEESE-AND-EGGS CAKE)

INGREDIENTS:

600 g flour, 2 eggs,
3 coffee cups oil, 1 cup yogurt, 1 teaspoon baking soda,
1 cup crumbed sirene (white cheese),
1 egg for glaze

1. Beat eggs, add oil, yogurt (with baking soda in it), crumbled cheese and flour.
2. Grease a baking pan, sprinkle with flour and pour in mixture. Brush surface with beaten egg. Bake in a moderate oven. If baked in hot oven, the cake becomes sodden.

ZELNIK
(BANITSA WITH SOUR CABBAGE)

INGREDIENTS:

1/2 kg flour, 1 cup lukewarm water, pinch of salt, 1 tablespoon vinegar;
for the filling – 1 small sour cabbage, 1 coffee cup melted lard (or oil);
2 coffee cups oil for greasing the pastry sheets

1. Make soft dough of water, salt, vinegar and flour. Knead.
2. Cut the well-kneaded dough in 12 balls and cover with a damp towel. Leave in a warm place for 1/2 hour.
3. Roll out balls in thin sheets. Cut sheets in four and bake each piece on a warm hot plate until lightly brown.
4. For the filling: chop sour cabbage and fry for a while in oil.
5. Put one layer of browned sheets in a greased baking pan, sprinkle with oil and some of the filling. Make 4–5 layers of sheets, sprinkled with oil and filling. Sprinkle the last layer just with oil.
6. Bake in a moderate oven.

TIKVENIK
(PUMPKIN PIE)

INGREDIENTS:

for the dough – 1 cup lukewarm water, 1 teaspoon oil,
1 tablespoon vinegar, pinch of salt, 1/2 kg flour;

for the filling – 1/2 kg pumpkin (peeled and seeds removed),
2 tablespoons oil, 3 tablespoons granulated sugar, 5 g cinnamon,
1 teaspoon salt, 1/2 cup crushed or ground walnuts;

2 coffee cups melted butter, 2–3 tablespoons powdered sugar

1. Make dough of flour, oil, vinegar, salt and water. Knead.
2. Cut dough in 20 balls and roll them out to the size of saucers. Grease each piece of rolled out dough with melted butter and join them by four to make five heaps.
3. Filling preparation: grate coarsely peeled pumpkin, sprinkle lightly with salt and leave for 1 hour. Then squeeze to drain juice, add oil, granulated sugar, cinnamon, salt and crushed walnuts.
4. Roll out four pastry sheets, 5 cm larger in diameter than the bottom of the baking pan. Put them one by one in the greased and floured baking pan, wrinkle and sprinkle with melted butter and some of the filling.
5. Roll out a fifth sheet with the same size as the baking pan, put it atop and pinch its ends with the ends of the sheets under it.
6. Cut pie in squares, sprinkle with melted butter and bake in a hot oven until brown.
7. Sprinkle with powdered (or granulated) sugar.

KOZUNAK (EASTER BREAD) WITH ALMONDS

INGREDIENTS:
1 kg flour, 4–5 eggs, 1 1/2 cups milk, 1/4 kg sugar,
1/2 teaspoon salt, 1/4 kg butter, 1 lemon, pinch of grated nutmeg,
2 tablespoons raisins,
1 egg for glaze,
2 tablespoons peeled almonds, yeast – the size of matchbox

1. Sift flour in a warm baking pan and make a well in the middle. Beat eggs, blend with milk, sugar and salt. Pour mixture gradually in the well, stirring with one hand. Add yeast diluted with water.

2. Knead dough, greasing hands now and then with melted butter. When dough is homogeneous, cover with a towel and leave in a warm place to rise until its volume doubles. Knead again with greased hands.

3. Add spices – lemon zest, grated nutmeg and raisins (scalded, dried and floured).

4. Put dough in a buttered baking pan and leave it to rise again. The risen dough should fill half of pan; otherwise it will rise too much during baking and will flow out of pan.

5. Brush top of bread with beaten egg. Stick in peeled off almonds (to peel them off more easily, scald almonds for a while, drain and rub with fingers one by one).

6. Bake in a moderate oven. Remove from baking pan when cooled.

7. Sprinkle with powdered sugar mixed with vanilla (optional).

MILK BANITSA

INGREDIENTS:

for the pastry sheets – 350 g flour, 1/2 teaspoon salt, 1 cup water;

250 g butter (or margarine) for greasing the pastry sheets;

for the milk mixture – 1 liter milk, 200 g sugar, 5 eggs, 2 g vanilla

1. Make dough of flour, salt and water, knead. Leave aside for 10–15 minutes, then roll in thin pastry sheets (See Home-made pastry sheets).

2. Put sheets in a buttered baking pan (preferably – rectangular), grease with melted butter using a brush, and cut in strips lengthwise.

3. Bake until golden.

4. Bring milk with sugar to boil, remove and blend with beaten eggs, stirring constantly. Add vanilla and pour mixture over the cooled baked sheets.

5. Return to oven and bake until mixture thickens. Cut in pieces and serve warm.

INZHIR BAKLAVA

INGREDIENTS:

3 cups flour, 3/4 cup water, 1 teaspoon salt,
200 g melted butter, 1 1/2 cups crushed walnuts;
for the syrup – 1/2 kg sugar, 2 cups water

1. Make dough of flour, salt and water. Knead.
2. Roll out 35–40 thin pastry sheets and leave to semi-dry.
3. Sprinkle each sheet with melted butter and walnuts, fold in a rectangular and roll on a thin rolling pin. One person holds the rolling pin and another person removes the sheet from it. Put rolled sheet in a greased baking pan and wind in a spiral.
4. Sprinkle with melted butter and bake in a moderate oven until lightly brown.
5. Prepare hot syrup of sugar and 2 cups water, and pour over cooled baklava.

SPONGE CAKE IN SYRUP

INGREDIENTS:

5 eggs, 5 tablespoons sugar, 2–3 g vanilla,
5 tablespoons flour, 200 g cream;
for the syrup – 600 g sugar, 2 cups water

1. Beat yolks with sugar and 1 coffee cup water in a saucepan on hot plate at low heat until sugar melts. Remove from heat and keep beating until mixture becomes white and cools down.
2. Fold in flour.
3. Beat whites until stiff and gently fold in mixture. Add vanilla and pour in a greased and floured baking pan.
4. Bake in a moderate oven. Poor over warm syrup prepared of sugar and 2 cups water. Leave to cool. Cut in squares.
5. Decorate each piece with a rose of cream.

BOILED WHEAT WITH MILK

INGREDIENTS:
1/2 kg wheat, 4 tablespoons flour,
3 tablespoons butter (or oil), 1/2 liter milk,
1 coffee cup grated walnuts, sugar

1. Boil wheat until the grains soften and crack.
2. Lightly brown flour in the oil until golden. Pour in the milk and simmer for about 20 minutes.
3. Add a few tablespoons wheat and stir well.
4. Pour mixture in boiled wheat and mix. Add walnuts and sugar to taste.

HONEY COOKIES

INGREDIENTS:
2 cups flour, 2 eggs, 2 tablespoons honey,
1 1/2 cups sugar, 1 cup oil, 1 teaspoon baking soda,
1 coffee cup walnuts

1. Knead on a table soft dough (it shouldn't be sticky) from beaten eggs, honey, sugar, oil, baking soda and flour.
2. Shape balls with the size of a walnut, decorate each ball with a walnut kernel.
3. Bake in a moderate oven until brown.

WALNUT COOKIES

INGREDIENTS:
3 egg whites, 1/4 kg sugar, 1/4 kg grated walnuts,
3–4 g vanilla, 2 coffee cups peeled almonds

1. Beat whites until stiff, fold in sugar and walnuts.
2. Put the saucepan with the mixture first on high heat, stirring constantly, then lower heat.
3. Remove from heat after 5–6 minutes and add vanilla. Leave to cool.

4. Shape balls the size of a walnut and decorate with almonds.

5. Arrange in a greased baking pan and bake in a moderate oven until lightly brown.

CHERRY PIE

INGREDIENTS:

1 coffee cup rice, 1 1/2 coffee cups water, 1 cup milk,
1 cup granulated sugar, 120 g butter, 1/4 kg powdered sugar, 3 eggs,
2 cups pitted cherries, pinch of cinnamon or vanilla,
1 coffee cup cherry jam,
powdered sugar for decoration

1. Cook rice in water. When the grains swell, add milk and granulated sugar. Leave to cool.

2. Mix very well butter with powdered sugar, add eggs one by one, stirring constantly, then pitted cherries and rice.

3. Pour the well-stirred mixture in a greased and floured baking pan. Bake in a moderate oven. Leave to cool.

4. Cut in pieces, sprinkle with powdered sugar, mixed with cinnamon (vanilla).

5. Decorate with cherry jam. Pour on cherry syrup (optional).

GRIS KHALVA (SEMOLINA KHALVA)

INGREDIENTS:

1/2 cup melted butter (or oil), 1 1/2 cups semolina, 1 cup sugar,
1/2 cup crushed or grated walnuts (or almonds),
1 coffee cup raisins, 1 tablespoon lemon juice, 2 cups water

1. Fry semolina in oil until golden, stirring constantly with an wooden spoon. Add walnuts (or almonds).

2. Add boiling syrup, prepared of sugar, water and lemon juice.

3. Put raisins and keep boiling, stirring constantly.

4. Remove from heat when mixture becomes homogeneous.

5. Pour khalva while still warm in a rectangular baking pan. Cut in pieces when cooled.

STEAMED PUMPKIN

INGREDIENTS:
1 medium pumpkin, honey, crushed walnuts, cinnamon

1. Cut pumpkin in two and remove seeds and fibers with a tablespoon.
2. Put a steaming net or an inverted plate in a saucepan. Cut pumpkin into pieces and arrange in saucepan with the rind down. Pour in water to cover the steaming net (or the plate) and steam at low heat until pumpkin is done. Add water if necessary.
3. When ready, scoop with a tablespoon the soft pulp and put into a deep dish.
4. Add honey to taste, crushed walnuts and cinnamon, and mix well.
Serve cold.

BELOVSKI STUFFED APPLES

INGREDIENTS:
1 1/4 kg apples, 1 1/2 coffee cups sugar,
2 coffee cups grated walnuts, 1 teaspoon cinnamon

1. Wash thoroughly apples, then hollow from the stem.
2. Stuff with mixture, prepared of sugar, walnuts and cinnamon, and arrange in a baking pan.
3. Bake in a moderate oven until soft.
Serve cold.

STRAWBERRY COMPOTE

INGREDIENTS:
1/2 kg strawberries;
for the syrup – 4 cups water, 6–7 tablespoons sugar

1. Select fresh ripe strawberries.
2. Prepare syrup of sugar and water.
3. Add strawberries and boil at moderate heat until soft.

4. Serve cold. The juice may be served separately as a soft drink.

Compote of apricots and other fruits may be prepared in the same way.

APRICOT JAM

INGREDIENTS:

1 kg apricots, 800 g sugar

1. Dissolve 1 tablespoon hydrated lime in 2 liters water and leave it to precipitate. Use cleared water.

2. Select and wash ripe apricots. Halve, pit and peel off.

3. Drop immediately in water with dissolved hydrated lime and leave for 1 1/2 hour.

4. Drain apricots, wash thoroughly with cold water and drop in boiling syrup, prepared of sugar and 1 cup water.

5. Boil for about 10 minutes, then remove apricots with a slotted spoon and continue boiling the syrup until thick.

6. Return apricots to syrup and boil until a drop of syrup makes a thread when squeezed between thumb and forefinger. Remove foam that comes out during boiling with a slotted spoon.

7. When ready, leave to cool for 12 hours and pour in dry jars.

GREEN FIGS JAM

INGREDIENTS:

800 g small green figs, 2 tablespoons salt of lemon, 2 kg sugar

1. Remove stems of figs, put in cold water and boil for 3–4 minutes; pour out water. Repeat this two more times, then pour in cold water.

2. Remove from water and pierce each fig with a thick needle. Drop in boiling syrup, made of sugar and 1 liter water.

3. After syrup comes to boil again, boil for 15 minutes, then remove from heat and leave to cool for about 10 hours.

4. Bring to boil again and boil until the figs soften. Remove from heat.

5. Add salt of lemon, dissolved in 2 coffee cups warm water.

GREEN WALNUTS JAM

INGREDIENTS:
1 kg green walnuts, 1 1/2 teaspoons salt of lemon, 1 kg sugar

1. Select young green walnuts that are easily pierced with a thick needle. Peel off, so that the white meaty body shows. Put in 0,5 % solution of tartaric acid (salt of lemon) to prevent from oxidation.

2. To remove the dark dying substances and bitter taste, drop walnuts in boiling water and boil for 5–6 minutes; pour out water. Repeat processing two more times. Cool for 15 minutes in cold water.

3. Drain and put in boiling syrup, made of sugar and 1 cup water.

4. Remove now and then the foam that comes out. Boil until the syrup thickens (a drop of it should remain whole when dropped on a cold porcelain plate).

5. When ready, add salt of lemon, dissolved in 1 1/2 coffee cups warm water.

Spices
used in the Bulgarian cuisine

Parsley – a garden plant. The leaves and roots are used as a spice. Parsley improves the proteins processing by the gastric juice and stimulates the gallic juice secretion. Use it fresh and add to the dishes just before serving, in order to preserve its high vitamin C content. Dry the leaves in a shady and airy place. Parsley roots are used as an addition to many dishes and also in some soups (for example, fish soup) during onion browning.

Mint – a garden plant used as a spice in many dishes – white beans soup and stew, stewed lamb, etc. Dry it in the same way as parsley.

Tarragon – a garden plant with leaves similar to those of the wormwood, with pleasant flavour, used as a spice and in medicine. Only its leaves are used, dried or fresh, with white beans soup, chicken soup and fish soup, stews, dishes with vegetables or fat meat, hen, turkey or game.

Cow-parsley – a perennial plant. Its roots, dried and ground, give the hot meals the same flavour as do its fresh leaves. It is used with soups and stews.

Dill – a perennial plant. The leaves have pleasant taste and strong flavour. It should be dried with the stem. Dill is used in the preparation of pickles. The chopped fresh leaves are used in dishes, made of early vegetables, green beans, zucchini, peas, broad beans, fresh cucumber salads, tarator, banitsa with filling of green plants' leaves, fish, hot soups, etc.

Thyme – a wild plant. Only its leaves are used (picked in late May or early June), dried in a shady and airy place. Frequently thyme is called *fish savoury* because, as it is said, *fish soup without thyme is no good.*

Savoury – a garden plant, growing on fertilized soil. It is sowed in early spring. Seedlings are grown first that are then planted. Savoury is picked in the summer, immediately after it blooms, and is then dried in a shady and airy place. For stronger flavour, bake it in an oven for a very short time and then crush the leaves and the seeds. Keep in glass jar with a tight lid. Savoury is also called *hen spice* as it is used in hen and chicken soups. It is used in the preparation of minced meat, in sausages, flat sausages and *lukanka* (special flat sausage), and in many stews.

Celery – a garden plant. Its leaves may be used fresh or dried. The roots are used in boiled dishes and stews; the leaves and stems (fresh or dried) – in stews and other dishes. It is used in the preparation of pickles – some of them are covered with a plait of celery stems with the leaves. The celery may be transferred to a pot in the autumn – cut the leaves, plant with the root up, and cover with soil. If kept in a warm place and regularly watered, it may be preserved for long during the winter.

Parsnip – a garden plant. The roots are used in boiled meals of fresh or canned vegetables.

Horse radish – a perennial plant with white succulent root. Its long leaves are used in the preparation of pickles. Grate the root, add salt, a pinch of sugar and pour in vinegar; thus prepared, the horse radish is served with boiled or roasted rich meats (especially, with boiled veal breasts), boiled veal tongue, and other meals. The baked and ground roots are used as a spice in hot meat soups.

Garlic – fresh or dried, crushed or in cloves, the garlic is used in many soups, stews, vegetable dishes, jelly, and fish, meat and poultry meals. Besides the spicy taste it gives to food, garlic is also an appetizer. When crushing it, first cut finely the cloves and add salt. Some meals are served with crushed garlic diluted with vinegar. A spicy salad is prepared with scalded green garlic. Scald just for a few minutes with lightly salted boiling water. Drain and cool. Cut and layer in a jar or in a sauce-pan, add parsley (with the stems), black peppercorns, dill and bay leaves, pour in solution of equal portions water used for the scalding, and vinegar. Keep in a cool place. When serving it, add some oil.

Basil – originally it comes from Persia and its name means *royal herb* (from the Greek *basilicus* – royal). Used in vegetable dishes; chopped basil leaves are used in the preparation of sauces. It gives a pleasant spicy flavour to soups with potatoes and especially with onion. Chopped fresh basil leaves are used in fish, meat and egg dishes; a flavoury vinegar, used for sauces and salads, is prepared with dill, basil and tarragon. Dried and ground basil seeds are an appropriate spice for sauces for meat, roasted on a rod, or for cold roasted meat.

Cumin – an annual ethereal oil plant (growing at wild or in gardens). Its flat fruits with small grains are used as a spice and in the medicine. Ground cumin is widely used in the preparation of sausages and salami of minced and chopped meat. Besides the imported one, there is cumin grown in the southern regions of Bulgaria. It stimulates digestive system's glands and increases appetite. If used in bigger quantities, cumin may cause stomach inflammation.

Oregano (marjoram) – a plant with tiny white and red flowers, used as a food spice.

This book was published with the kind assistance of:

Kachin Agency

Sofia, Bulgaria

**High quality translating
and interpreting services !**

Tel. 0359 2/ 466 053, 444 600
E-mail: interpre@mail.techno-link.com

Bulgarian Cuisine
The best traditional recipes
By Dimitar Mantov

Lay-out: Pavel Sotirov
Translated by: Dimitar Stavrev
Edited by: Panayot Spirov

May Publishing House

Bulgaria, Sofia 1000, Vasil Levski street 21
Tel./Fax: 00359-2-981 7682
E-mail: may@techno-link.com